Do you know w [...] read but deeply powerful [...] bbie has laid his finger or [...] tian life: we worship, serve, give, and otherwise follow Christ, but we do so without passion, and for this reason we have so many competing interests that our commitment to Christ is diluted. We have the form without the power, the words but not the burden, the doctrine but not the reality. I want to reread this book when it is published and I will recommend it to my congregation as well.

**—Dr. Erwin W. Lutzer**
**Senior Pastor, The Moody Church**
**Chicago, IL**

In his helpful book, *Passion Cry*, Pastor Robbie Symons leads us to understand that heat must accompany light—that truth without spirit, head without heart, leads inevitably to a "shoulders up" faith where followers become fearful fact-checkers and lose the fervency that makes following Christ truly fulfilling. Robbie Symons has been used of God to plant and build one of the greatest churches in North America, a fellowship that combines precept and passion in a truly compelling way.

If you want fresh passion for the purposes of the Lord in your life, you are holding a book on that topic written by a man who lives it and wants to help you get there, too. Read it carefully and apply it faithfully and your life in Christ will soar to new heights.

**—James MacDonald**
**Senior Pastor, Harvest Bible Chapel**
**Chicago, IL**

If Christianity is worth anything, it is worth everything. Robbie Symons' soul has been arrested by the passion of Christ—both as a disciple and a pastor. He communicates this passion better than anyone I know. *Passion Cry* is an incredibly powerful and practical distillation of biblical zeal that will eradicate apathy and equip you to live a fulfilling and fruitful Christian life.

**—Daniel Henderson**
**President, Strategic Renewal International**
**National Director, The 6:4 Fellowship**
**Denver, CO**

I love this book. It is clear, practical, vital, and urgent. It speaks to such a need in my life and the life of the church to kindle afresh our first love for Jesus. Nothing significant or vital gets done without deep, energizing convictions coming to life. Robbie has lived out this teaching on the passionate pursuit of Jesus as long as I have known him. This is a powerful book because it has a powerful message.

—Kent Shaw
**Executive Director, Harvest Bible Fellowship**
**Elgin, IL**

Every Christ follower who desires a deeper passion for the Lord should read this book. Robbie masterfully peels back the layers of the heart, exposing dispassion and challenging readers to a fresh and fervent pursuit of their Savior. As you read this book, you will find yourself crying out, "As a deer pants for flowing streams, so pants my soul for you, Oh God" (see Psalm 42:1). Once you pick this book up, you won't put it down.

—Bill Borinstein
**Senior Pastor, Harvest Bible Chapel**
**Phoenix, AZ**

If you want to ignite a deep passion for Christ, this is the book for you. Robbie is my pastor, friend, and a genuine, passionate man of God. He lives what he preaches and he is truly discontent with spiritual contentment. This book will powerfully reinvigorate your life in Christ. I highly recommend *Passion Cry*.

—James Reimer
**NHL Goaltender**
**Toronto, ON**

HOW APATHY IS KILLING THE CHURCH
AND HOW PASSION FOR CHRIST WILL REVIVE IT

# PASSION CRY

# ROBBIE SYMONS
FOREWORD BY JAMES MACDONALD

Printed in Canada

ISBN: 978-1-4866-1269-7

Word Alive Press
131 Cordite Road, Winnipeg, MB R3W 1S1
www.wordalivepress.ca

MIX
Paper from
responsible sources
FSC® C016245

Cataloguing in Publication information may be obtained through Library and Archives Canada.

*To my four children, affectionately known as "the circus."*
*Aidan, Cale, Sadie, and Bliss.*
*May your ultimate passion be His passion for His glory.*
*Dad loves you!*

# Acknowledgements

Iam humbled and deeply grateful for the people the Lord has used over the years to shape my heart, and it is my delight to honour their impact on my life.

To my parents, who demonstrated unconditional love, grace, and patience towards me. You provided a home where the seeds of passion for Christ could take root. I love you. To my precious bride, Gillian, you are my greatest gift and blessing in life and ministry. Your love, support, and strength in Christ have fuelled my passion for more of Him. We both know there is no way I would have made it this far without you.

To the elders of Harvest Bible Chapel Oakville, I thank God for you all. You are friends, mentors, and wisdom personified. For the many times you have held up my arms in the battle, for sharing my passion for the things that matter most, I thank you. To our Harvest Oakville staff, you are a tremendous team whom I immensely value. Thank you for your dedication to the Lord. To the people of Harvest Oakville, it is pure joy to serve Jesus Christ with you. I love how God is transforming us, and I count it great joy to be surrounded by such receptive and humble people. Your passion for Christ inspires me. You are loved so very much.

To A.W. Tozer, who set a path and course of passion for God that has greatly impacted me over many years, I am so thankful for your life and how God is using your story and insight to inspire the next generation.

To pastor James MacDonald, who shares my passion for planting churches for the glory of God, thank you for your investment in my life.

To Stacey Weeks and Neil Wilson, who made this book possible through encouragement, editing, consultation, and a lot of hard work; Karen Higginson, who supported this project and covered it in prayer; and my assistant Maureen Kelly, who has served and supported me with such humility and excellence. To Word Alive Press and to the many others who believed in this project from the very beginning, your encouragement and faith was the difference maker in bringing this book to print.

To my Saviour, Jesus Christ, thank you for saving me. The moment You opened my eyes to spiritual reality, You infused me with a passion for Your beauty and glory. You are my greatest treasure and my greatest satisfaction. I love You, Lord Jesus. This is for You.

# Foreword

The facts that undergird Christianity are the biblical doctrines forged through centuries of biblical scholarship. The truths of what the Bible teaches—the nature and work of Jesus Christ, His atoning death and resurrection, God's triune nature, etc.— are settled in the minds of serious Bible students. However, what remains is to see those truths come to life. If right believing alone was going to fulfill the Great Commission, the job Christ gave us would have been done long ago.

In *Passion Cry*, Pastor Robbie Symons leads us to understand that heat must accompany light—that truth without spirit, head without heart, leads inevitably to a "shoulders up" faith where followers become fearful fact-checkers and lose the fervency that makes following Christ truly fulfilling. Robbie Symons has been used of God to plant and build one of the greatest churches in North America, a fellowship that combines precept and passion in a truly compelling way.

God is surely passionate about His Son, His universe, and His saving power. If you have lost the passion of your Father in heaven and long to feel your faith in deeper ways, if you want fresh passion for the purposes of the Lord in your life, you are holding a book on that topic written by a man who lives it and wants to help you get there, too. Read it carefully, apply it faithfully, and your life in Christ will soar to new heights.

—James MacDonald
Senior Pastor Harvest Bible Chapel
Chicago, IL

## INTRODUCTION
Why a Book on Passion?

Nothing is so effective in keeping true Christianity alive as the yeast of zealous Christians scattered throughout the Church.[1]

—J.C. Ryle

*Do not be slothful in zeal, be fervent in spirit, serve the Lord.*

—Romans 12:11

God loves passion… passion for Him. This truth is both undeniable and irrefutable, according to Scripture. The Word of God reveals a holy God who is unashamedly jealous for the love of His people, and this is because when He has the love of His people, He has the passion of His people and He is most glorified in His people. This sincere passion for God is ultimately rooted in the comprehension and application of the gospel. If we truly see the treasure, we cannot stop the zeal (Philippians 3:8).

Christian passion is a burning desire to please the Lord in how we think and live. This zeal cannot be produced by the flesh of man, but is a supernatural longing created by the Holy

Spirit at conversion. The passionate pursuit of God quenches our greatest thirst and satisfies our deepest hunger. But here's the question: why do so many believers lack this zeal? Why is genuine passion for Christ seemingly so rare and apathy so common? Why is there such a malaise upon the bride of Christ in a day when true passion has never been so needed?

Passion holds an indispensable role within the disciple of Christ. As genuine followers of Christ, we simply cannot afford to live without passion for Him. It's that essential. J.C. Ryle, a man who understood with incredible clarity the importance of passion within the Church, said, "It is impossible to overestimate the debt that all Christians owe to zeal."[2] He was pointing out the unavoidable truth that our passions define us, drive us, and distinguish us. This fact applies to everyone, not just Christ-followers.

Consider the role of passion in the lives of great leaders throughout history. Examine the motivations and trajectory of Alexander the Great, Julius Caesar, and Napoleon, to name just a few. Their drive and incredible accomplishments were fuelled by their single-minded passion and zeal. Even the bad boys of history, like Hitler and Stalin, displayed shocking passion for their goals, though it was insanely self-centred and disconnected from any acknowledgment of God.

The impact of one's life has always been shaped by the desire and passion that drives them, whether for good or ill. How much more should followers of Christ be filled with passion for Him who holds true, joy-filled, and everlasting life?

Contemplate the impact of the apostles and their all-out, passionate pursuit of Jesus Christ. They were so convinced of the true worth of Christ that they literally forsook all that prevented their service for Him, and often gave their lives as a result.

Review the record of the early Church and the impact of their passion. They held a resolute conviction to see the gospel spread as far as God would take them. They endured immense persecution and life-threatening trials, yet their undivided desire to honour Christ spurred them to mind-blowing fruitfulness in the power of the Holy Spirit.

Consider the burning passion of reformers like Wycliffe, Tyndale, and Luther. Each displayed an inspiring and contagious conviction for the glory of God and His gospel. But what drove them? Their fervent undying pursuit of the Lord and His kingdom.

Consider the society-changing impact of puritans like Owen, Edwards, and Baxter. Consider the revival-producing fruit of the preaching of Whitefield, Wesley, and Spurgeon. Consider the world-altering sacrifice of missionaries like Hudson Taylor, Adoniram Judson, and John G. Paton. What allowed these men to be used with such extended fruitfulness that it's still bearing fruit hundreds of years later? The answer is a passionate, burning desire for the Lord Jesus Christ and His glory, rooted in the comprehension and application of the gospel. They knew the treasure and could not stop the zeal. This kind of fruit simply cannot be accomplished apart from a powerful appetite for God.

Are we any different today? I believe that apathy is killing the Church, because many who claim to know Jesus do not understand or apply the life-changing truth of the gospel—and because they do not know the treasure of the gospel, they lack zeal. Nothing can replace the impact of a passionate pursuit of God.

Can we ever truly overestimate the influence of true and pure passion upon the Church? I am not talking about a passion filled with fanatical displays of emotion. I'm talking about a passion fuelled by the glory of God. I'm talking about a conviction for eternal treasures, a decreasing self, and an increasing Christ. We know without question that the Lord loves to honour those who passionately pursue Him. The Lord Almighty has always held up, honoured, and used powerfully those who hearts are fully committed to Him.

Just think of the impact of David, a man after God's heart (Acts 13:22). Just think of the greatest commandment (Matthew 22:37–39) and the inherent passion and zeal that is found within. Just think of the call for our first love (Revelation 2:4), the despising of lukewarm affection (Revelation 3:16), and the command for single-minded and all-out devotion (Philippians 3:8). Just think of Romans 12:11, which says, *"Do not be slothful in zeal, be fervent in spirit..."*

The Church has suffered too long from the pressure to conform to the dull, lukewarm, disinterested, and dispassionate status quo approach to Christ. I pray that day is done. I pray that the tide will turn and a new normal will be written, that the peer pressure within the Church will turn towards a heat-producing zeal for the Lord Jesus Christ. I pray that instead of apathy, we would see an awakening of contagious Christianity fuelled by a passionate love of our Saviour. There is no way to deny that this is what the Lord has chosen to use over the history of the Church, and what He will continue to use in our day.

Is there any more important call upon the Church today? In the face of tremendous societal pressure, cultural and moral revolution, and an anti-Christ flavour increasing with every day, what will God's people do? Has there been another time in recent memory when it was so important for the Church to rise up and decide which flag we are truly going to fly? As the persecution upon Christ-followers moves from subtle to not-so-subtle, we are about to find out where our passions really lie. That is why this message is so needed.

As we begin this passionate pursuit of passion for Christ, allow me to show you how to get the most from this book. Each chapter is part of a greater whole yet designed to stand alone to encourage you at a particular point of time or interest. Do not be afraid to read slowly and maximize each chapter. I also encourage you, when prompted by the Holy Spirit, to stop, consider, and pray through the truth you are encouraged and/ or convicted by. The most fruit will come from this approach.

When you understand the treasure of the gospel and apply the resulting life-changing truths, genuine passion for God will follow. May the Lord choose to ignite a fire in us that produces undeniable fruit from our lives!

**CHAPTER ONE**
How I Stumbled into Passion

*…for at one time you were darkness, but now you are light in the Lord. Walk as children of light…*
—Ephesians 5:8

If Christ be anything he must be everything. O rest not till love and faith in Jesus be the master passions of your soul![3]
—Charles Spurgeon

March 9, 1997 started out as the worst day of my life. That Sunday morning, I found myself alone in my parents' house flooded with discouragement and deep despair. I felt completely lost and confused. I was angry and I had no answers. I had spent the previous two days at different universities visiting friends and seeking to satisfy myself with what had captured my heart for years. I had recently graduated from university, but the campus party scene and the need to hear others affirm my identity pulled me like a magnet back to my alma mater. I was there to get what I always got: self-fulfillment, self-gratification, and self-indulgence. Whether through partying, socializing, or seeking worldly success, the source didn't really matter because the combination had always worked… at least until now.

I still remember the vivid scene. I was in a campus bar, music blaring, place packed, everyone dancing, talking, and laughing. This was the atmosphere I lived for, that I longed for. But something happened that night, a reaction I had never experienced before. I was standing in the middle of hundreds of people, surrounded by the lights, sounds, and smells of entertainment, with friends I thought cared for and welcomed me.

But then it hit me: I felt alone, so desperately alone. At that moment, it was like the world stood still and I could no longer hear music or people talking. I froze and something inside me said, *"Robbie, what are you doing here?"* The incredibly strange occurrence stunned me. I listened, I paused, and then I left. I didn't say goodbye to anyone; I just pushed my way through the crowd, walked out the door, and went to my car.

Something was happening to me, but I had no idea what.

I chalked up the oddity to a bad night, so I drove to another university about an hour away. But this experience was worse than the first. I spent the night with strangers, and I distinctly remember my misery and frustration as torment flooded my thoughts. I spent hours that night agonizing over my predicament. I couldn't explain it, didn't understand it, and couldn't escape the feeling that my soul was in trouble.

During this crisis, I wrestled with questions I could not answer. I looked ahead and noticed how much of what I was doing was actually searching for meaning, purpose, and fulfillment. I had a lot to be thankful for, significant successes in the world's terms, and great prospects to look forward to—or so I thought. But as I watched the world around me, as I considered the philosophy of what I had been taught, as

I questioned the goals of my friends and peers, it all seemed wrong. I suddenly saw myself as part of a crowd headed in a direction I increasingly felt I didn't want to take. I began to despise the world, and more importantly, despise myself and all that I stood for.

With little sleep and much anguish, I got up that Sunday morning and drove home. I spent most of that two-hour drive in frustrated tears. What was wrong with me? Why did I feel this way? Why did all the things that used to fulfill me suddenly seem so empty? Why did my own desires repulse me? Why did I hate myself, hate my behaviour? I was starting to see that there was a hole in my heart much larger than I had ever wanted to admit. Hopelessness quickly settled in.

During that early morning car ride, I called out and cried with great anger. I wept at the realization of how needy and broken I was. Even more devastating was facing the fact that I was a disaster, but I had no solution to the plague consuming my own soul.

Now that is an empty feeling.

I arrived at my parents' empty house. They were already at church, my older sister was away at school, and my younger brother was on a school trip. I was home, but alone, miserable, and consumed with darkness. The last thing I expected was for that moment to change my life forever. My darkness was about to be confronted by the Light.

Earlier that year, my brother had gone to a Christian summer camp. During his trip, he had picked up some Christian music and encouraged me to listen to it. I, of course, was way too cool for Christian music, so I paid little attention... until now. The particular CD must have sat by the player for months, undisturbed and collecting dust. However, in my moment of desperation and agony of soul, I was open to anything.

I remember thinking, or even saying out loud, "God, if you're really there, then I'm willing to listen, because I am coming undone."

The CD was by DC Talk, a popular Christian band at the time. I put it in the player, and because I was so clueless about what song to play, I hit the random button. Song #10 came up. Vaguely curious, I opened the CD jacket and began to follow the words, not prepared for the tidal wave of grace that was about to be poured on me. This was to be my gospel moment.

You need to know that I was raised on the message of Christ in a great home with a great family. But because the gospel wasn't about me, I didn't have any real attraction or time for it. The good news about God's love and His plan was around me so constantly that I ignored it. Sure, I believed in God, but I didn't know Him—and I knew it. I went through the motions: I sang in the junior choir, was confirmed as a thirteen-year-old, and even served as an altar boy in the Anglican Church, but I never *really* knew Him. I never met the One this was all about.

The strangest part, looking back, is that I believed God was real to the point that I defended Him to my friends, all the while actually being afraid Christ might return because I knew down deep that I wasn't going to heaven. But don't get me wrong: those moments of honest realization were few and far between. Everything else about my life was a passionate desire to serve self, love self, and worship self.

But on this day, I was approaching the place of recognizing that my frantic pursuit of self would always go wrong. Always!

The song played. I followed along with the lyrics, and each word stabbed my soul. Sentence after sentence, the artist sang about my self-seeking, self-centred excuse of a life.

It was my whole life thus far put to music: a passionate pursuit of life apart from God, apart from Christ. My existence was a self-driven, pride-filled, insatiable appetite for the world as it related to me and I constantly justified it in my own reasoning. The word "selfish" hit me hard. But the song kept going, questioning my motives and perfectly expressing what I had been crying out in agony just an hour before in the car: *I hate who I've become, but why I am no longer fulfilled? Why do I feel this way? Why all of a sudden do I despise who I am and what I am about?*

As these shattering questions echoed in my mind, the next line in the song held the answer I had been afraid I wouldn't find. I needed a Saviour.

It's really difficult for me to describe what happened next. As I said, this was my gospel moment. This was the flashpoint of my regeneration and conversion. This was the crisis after which I would never be the same again, ever. The instant that line was sung, and as I read the words in the CD jacket,[4] I knew I had my answer… to everything. And I mean everything!

The closest story in Scripture I can relate to my experience is what happened to the radical, driven, self-seeking Pharisee named Saul on the road to Damascus.

> *Now as [Saul] went on his way, he approached Damascus, and suddenly a light from heaven shone around him. And falling to the ground he heard a voice saying to him, "Saul, Saul, why are you persecuting me?" And he said, "Who are you, Lord?" And he said, "I am Jesus…"* (Acts 9:3–5)

On that Sunday morning, on the road to despair, light from heaven flashed around me, at least spiritually speaking. In a moment I was crushed with the awesome love of God. The gospel I had heard all my life in some form or another, but which I had never understood or applied, was instantly made real to my heart. The scales were lifted, my eyes were opened, my heart felt, and my soul became alive with a power that could not be stopped. The longing of my heart, the torment of my soul, the hopelessness of my mind were all answered. Everything that had been chaos in my life was completely and supernaturally settled.

Tears formed and cries rose from my lungs. But these were now tears of joy and sobs of relief and gratitude. True, unadulterated worship from my heart for the first time in my life. I could see! I could see!

I kid you not, I cried at the top of my lungs for an hour straight. I cried with joy, I sang with praise, I felt and knew the worship of my Saviour for the first time in my existence. I realized why I was alive and I knew my purpose. I had the answer to my misery and the solution to my devastation of sin. His name is Jesus Christ!

I must have listened to that song twenty times in a row, and sang it louder and louder each time it played. Why? Because a passion had been born in me. I truly saw the treasure of Christ for the first time. My eyes were opened and my heart kindled for Christ.

As I sang and cried and sang and cried some more, I looked in the mirror at my tear-stained but smiling face, repeatedly saying, "It just makes sense." What made sense? The gospel! Everything, in that moment, made sense to me. All the teaching, all the Sunday school memories, all the family devotions, all the Bible studies, all the testimonies over the years instantly made sense. Me! I was a sinner in need of a Saviour! Jesus had died for *my* sin and Jesus loved me!

That was the unexpected moment when I received the gift of His grace through faith—and, well, life would never be the same again. *I* would never be the same again. A passion was born in me, a passion for the light of Christ! My former pursuit of pleasure and self-fulfillment was suddenly a memory of lost and purposeless wandering.

At this astounding, mind-blowing, life-changing moment, the words of Charles Wesley's beautiful hymn describe my experience perfectly:

> Long my imprisoned spirit lay,
> Fast bound in sin and nature's night;
> Thine eye diffused a quickening ray—
> I woke, the dungeon flamed with light;
> My chains fell off, my heart was free,
> I rose, went forth, and followed Thee.[5]

That's just it. "I woke, the dungeon flamed with light." Oh, how incredible and marvellous to consider the reality of salvation in Jesus Christ. The chains fell off and my heart was free! Even as I write this all these years later, my mind is renewed and my heart leaps with joy over the reality of being rescued from sin and forever being alive in Jesus Christ.

You see, the moment a sinner truly awakens and stares at the cross of Jesus Christ, recognizing that his or her sin put Jesus there, is a doorway to amazing change. When a sinner suddenly understands that on the cross Jesus Christ took on their penalty and punishment in their places so they might live? That's the lightning bolt when all hell breaks loose. The chains are broken, the shackles slip off, and the prison door swings wide open. In that moment, the sinner is set free and true life and love take up permanent residence. All that supernatural change sparks a time of heavenly elation and unspeakable joy, and that's the wonderful crisis where true passion begins, a passion unlike any other.

It's a passion that the world cannot understand, fuelled by love, spurred on by hope, and carried by faith. It only makes sense when you realize where it comes from and who keeps it fuelled. Ephesians 5:8 says, *"for at one time you were darkness, but now you are light in the Lord"* (emphasis added). On March 9, 1997, I woke in darkness. I *was* darkness. I was sentenced to death. Under God's wrath, I was headed for hell. But only a few hours later, by the wonders of the love of God and the grace found only in Jesus Christ, I became light!

Today, if you are saved in Jesus Christ, your story is no different. You *were* darkness, but now you are light in the Lord! Consider the magnitude of this truth. Doesn't this fire you up? Have you forgotten how darkness consumed you, but then light rescued you? How darkness blinded you, but then light transformed you? When darkness imprisoned you, but then light freed you? When darkness hated you, but then light loved you? Tell me, should we, as those who *are* light, have a powerful passion and unending devotion for the light? The answer is yes!

All those years ago, for reasons I cannot fully explain, the Lord Jesus Christ showed me the light and made me to be light. From that point on, I have been fully called to an undying passion for the light. God's grace that day absolutely proved to me that everything else in life is loss compared to the surpassing worth of knowing Christ Jesus my Lord (Philippians 3:8).

What are we waiting for? Enough with the games, enough with the half-hearted Christian dabbling, enough with complacent, apathetic living. Enough! Enough of believers displaying passion for everything but the light. Enough of the pursuit of temporal trinkets. Enough of obsessive self-indulgence. Enough of being lured by darkness, because in Christ we've been saved from that (Colossians 1:13)!

We have been saved by the light, so it is time to call down a passion for the light—passion that is rooted in truth, and a truth that leads to zeal.

**CHAPTER TWO**

The Mission of Passion: More

*Oh, taste and see that the Lord is good!*

—Psalm 34:8

The man is "saved" but he is not hungry nor thirsty after God. In fact, he is specifically taught to be satisfied and is encouraged to be content with little.[6]

—A.W. Tozer

"I bet you can't eat just one!" Do you know the commercial I'm referring to? A marketing department dreamed up this line to sell potato chips. It contains the idea that once you've tried and tasted one of their potato chips, you'll be hooked and crave more. And for a lot of people, they're right. We all know the feeling of placing into our mouths our favourite food or dessert—that jolt when the taste buds light up and signal to our brain that we've just tasted something very yummy. It then gives us the order to do it again, and often we keep doing it until another signal hits the brain: "Stop, I'm bloated."

But that only relates to the taste of temporal and fleeting food. What about the taste of the eternal, all-satisfying, and flat-out awesome Lord? Psalm 34:8 says, *"Oh, taste and see that the Lord is good!"* The reality of that first Sunday morning of my spiritual rebirth meant I was given a meal that I hadn't even known was possible. I experienced a taste, an enjoyment, a satisfaction above all others. It was truly supernatural and remarkable, a spiritual feast spread out before me that included the tastes of eternal life, of the riches and inheritance of Christ, of the fellowship of the Holy Spirit, and of the love of the Father enveloping me. But I distinctly remember most the unparalleled satisfaction of receiving what God offered to me. Oh the satisfaction!

The world had let me down for twenty-two years. All the promises of fulfillment through personal accomplishment, obsessive idolatry, lusting after flesh, and insatiable pride had come up empty. The world couldn't deliver on its promises. Every single time I would go after the next "thing," hoping and dreaming of a better future and happiness, I was left worse off than before.

That's the deception and hollow nature of the world. It's like a donut. Sure, it tastes really good at first, but in the end it's empty of any real nutrition. To encounter the living God, to taste and see that the Lord is good, literally changed everything for me. Once you've truly tasted the Lord and heaven, trust me: you cannot stop the zeal.

### SURPASSING WORTH

Taste and satisfaction are why the apostle Paul said, *"I count everything as loss because of the surpassing worth of knowing Christ Jesus my Lord"* (Philippians 3:8). He had tried the world; he had gone after the promises and desires of his own heart. He had thought he was accomplishing it all, but in the end he met Jesus and everything else became dung.

That is the power of tasting that the Lord is so good. Nothing else even comes close. Satisfaction is the call and life of the true believer in Jesus Christ.

You and I have been called to so much more. We've been saved for so much more. Shouldn't we then desire so much more? How can we revert to idols when we've been given the right to become children of God?

Again, this is a serious call for passion. Hear this as a call resulting from our reality in Christ. We need a deeper level of intensity for the truth of the gospel. The world waits to see in those who claim to follow Jesus a passion for the only One who matters. They need to see us giving our very lives for what moth and rust cannot destroy. How can we respond with anything less than passion for that which has given us true and abundant life? This is a call to unleash unapologetic passion for the only thing we will actually care about the moment we cease to live on this earth.

## ONE SECOND AFTER DEATH

The moment you pass from this life, you will not give one nanosecond of thought to the temporal things of this earth. Not one. Do you realize this? As someone who lives in Christ and by Christ, I know this to be true. I believe it with all my heart.

Well then, what in the world is wrong with me so often? Why do I get all concerned, worried, frantic, and idolatrous over things that have no value? Why do I get lured back into the traps of emptiness, shallowness, and futility? It's because I lose perspective of what actually holds value, what actually counts. This persistent failure reminds me of a little poem by C.T. Studd:

> Only one life, t'will soon be past
> Only what's done for Christ will last[7]

Please understand me. The motivation here is not to earn points with God; the motivation is to truly keep tasting and feeding on the life which is only found in Christ. I long to know that all-satisfying taste of the Lord Jesus Christ that becomes the only item on my menu. Unlike other meals, which can become boring or mundane after a while, you will never—and I mean never—become bored of the taste of Jesus Christ. You will want more and more and more; He is that satisfying and awesome!

I have marvelled in recent weeks and months at the goodness and satisfaction of my Saviour. It blows me away how good He tastes. The world can't match it, the pagans don't know it, and the devil is terrified of it, because He tastes *so* good! To be filled with His presence, to be saturated in His love, to be infused with His gospel! Oh the joy, the tears, the gladness, and satisfaction of the soul. Oh, taste and see that the Lord is good! This is why John G. Paton, the inspiring missionary to cannibals, said, "Those who have tasted this highest joy, 'the joy of the Lord', will never again ask—'Is life worth living?'"[8]

This is precisely why Peter says in 1 Peter 2:2–3, "*Like newborn infants, long for the pure spiritual milk, that by it you may grow up to salvation—if indeed you have tasted that the Lord is good*" (emphasis added). And why is this so important? Because we always feed ourselves on that which makes us hungry. The reason you go to the fridge and pick out your favourite sandwich is because you hunger for it. The reason you sit down each week and watch your favourite TV show is because you hunger for it. And the reason you make time for your Saviour and speak to Him and love Him is because you hunger for *Him*.

## DON'T TRY HARDER; LOVE MORE

Understand that this is ultimately not about trying harder and becoming more religious in nature. This is not a call for passion that imitates pharisaic attitudes of self-righteousness. Not at all. This is rather a call to love!

When you've truly tasted the Lord, you know His love, and there's nothing like it. You hunger for Him because you understand the gospel. When you've tasted the goodness of His love, you want more because nothing equates with His love and grace and intimacy.

This is not about playing a religious game so God will pat you on the back and say "good boy" or "good girl." Rather, this is about becoming more and more aware of the unconditional love of the Father upon your undeserving soul and the sacrificial love of your Redeemer to the point that you can't help but want to give your whole life in return. That is the gospel. What response is there other than zeal? Lethargy? Complacency? God help us, no! It cannot be. When we truly taste of the grace of the life-giving gospel, we are filled with a passion for more. More of Him!

You see, because God loves us so much, He will not allow us to stay where we are. Therefore, by His grace and because of His grace He calls us to more of Himself, because that is where we are most satisfied and He is most glorified. (John Piper just said "Amen.")

At times throughout this book, you'll feel some conviction (truth). Just don't let it turn to self-condemnation (a lie). A huge part of why you're even holding this book is because the Lord wants to do more in you. So again, do not receive this as an attempt to push you to try harder to accomplish some human-set goal or agenda. Receive this is a call for passionate love in response to the inexhaustible grace that has been placed upon you as a blood-bought child of God.

## THE GREATEST COMMANDMENT

I often think we make the will of God far too complicated. We get caught up in so many details of life and become filled with anxiety over the decisions before us. Now, I'm not downplaying the importance of career, marriage, or what city we should live in. However, if we're seeking to see God's will only in these matters, we will miss the big picture—and miss out greatly.

My advice in preaching and to individuals is often to start with what we know. When it comes to the will of God, what do we know to be a hundred percent His will? Well, how about start with the first and greatest commandment of all? Jesus answered that question: *"You shall love the Lord your God with all your heart and with all your soul and with all your mind. This is the great and first commandment"* (Matthew 22:37–38). How clear is that? I certainly consider myself a simple guy in a lot of ways, but this is where I love simplicity. Before we get all caught up in the complexities of life, how about we start with what comes first? Love God... passionately!

You want to know the will of God for your life? Here it is, guaranteed. Love the Lord with all your heart and with all your soul and with all your mind. Instead of spending the next month frantically pacing about circumstances of life, how about taking the next month to passionately pursue the Father with love?

Listen, it's the greatest commandment for a reason. It matters! This is when a true passion for the light becomes a true passion for more, because He is all there truly is. So that's where our love is to truly go!

## PYRAMID OF GLASSES

When the Lord transformed my life and filled me with a passion for Him, He showed me something early on: our lives are like a pyramid of glasses. This may sound odd to you, but stay with me.

Imagine a pyramid of stemware glasses, the sort often used to create a champagne fountain. I'm not a champagne guy, but I do appreciate how the pyramid works. You fill the top glass until it overflows and the liquid begins to fill the second row of glasses, and so on. This keeps going until all the glasses in all the rows are filled from the source. It's a beautiful thing to watch in many respects. But what's way more beautiful is when Jesus Christ is your top glass. If you seek to fill your life with Jesus Christ and a passion for Him, you are guaranteed that every other glass will be filled with Him. However, if you start to fill certain sections of the pyramid without starting at the top, certain glasses will remain empty and unfulfilled. With Christ as your top glass, you can't go wrong.

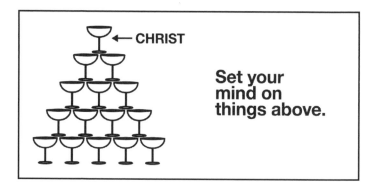

← CHRIST

**Set your mind on things above.**

If the pyramid represents our lives, and if Christ is our top glass and loving Him is our source, then every single glass will be filled with Christ Himself! This is why passages like Colossians 3:1 are so profound: *"If then you have been raised with Christ, seek the things that are above, where Christ is, seated at the right hand of God."* This is also why verses such as Matthew 6:33 become oh so very powerfully true: *"But seek first the kingdom of God and his righteousness, and all these things will be added to you."* The power and point of this verse is to *seek first* the kingdom of God.

Seeking first the kingdom is filling your top glass with Jesus Christ. As you begin with Him, inevitably you end with Him; it's just good theology. Think of the context found in Matthew 6. Jesus is speaking about combatting worry and anxiety by having faith for the provision of God. Consider then how much time, energy, and anguish we spend on worry, anxiety, and wondering what the will of God is for our lives. You see, when your first passion is Christ and your top glass is filled with Him, His truth, thoughts, and power will automatically begin to flow down into your life.

As I love to tell myself and others, "Try this for a month and then get back to me." Try to earnestly and honestly seek first the kingdom. With simplicity and sincerity, seek to pursue a passionate love for Christ. How? It's nothing new, but completely new at the same time.

This very morning, I found myself a little frantic with details of the world, busyness at home, and distractions calling for the attention of my heart. Here I can start to feel tension in my soul and disquiet in my heart. If left unchecked, it will almost always undermine my strength, my effort, my volition, and ultimately my will. I don't want that. Not at all. So what do I do? All I know to do: seek first the kingdom, setting my mind on things above. I fill my top glass with the riches and love of my Saviour.

This seeking is done through His Word. Where else can I start? The seeking continues through prayer and confession of the very sins that have side-tracked my heart. I also seek the kingdom through musical worship. Musical worship is such a beautiful gift from God, releasing our hearts to sing words of truth that renew our minds and spark a passion of affection from within. Then I prioritize Christ's kingdom through journaling, which places on paper the thoughts I receive, the wisdom I gather, and the direction I'm headed in my pursuit of His will. I'm living in His kingdom when I genuinely take all these pursuits of passion and turn them into a prayer for the day ahead. I turn them into a powerful opportunity for a Spirit-filled and Christ-centred day. This is when I seriously start to believe and see the potential for so much more!

## MISSION STATEMENT FOR MORE

As I look back on my conversion, the change was so night and day. One second I was shrouded in darkness, and the next moment I was consumed with the light of Christ. The transformation was so powerful, so real, so overwhelming! And the change in me touched off a volcano of expectation for grace, for transformation in other people's lives. I very quickly began to believe just how much God is in the business of transformation. After all, that's the point of the gospel: life change for the glory of God.

By God's grace, a fire in me had been kindled with passion for Jesus that was not about to go out anytime soon. But the most interesting part is that when I described this fire—really, this expectation for transformation in Christ—to other believers, I often received blank or awkward stares. I quickly began to realize that within the Western Church, there is an unhealthy contentment.

As I learned early on from one of my favourite authors, A.W. Tozer, material contentment is good, but spiritual contentment is bad. The moment believers become spiritually content is the moment they go backwards in their walk with Christ. I've learned that satisfaction in Christ is not a static thing; true satisfaction in Christ leaves us hungry and yearning for more, every day and every step of the way. There is no neutrality in

Christian faith: you're either going forwards or backwards. This is why spiritual passion and expectation are everything.

One of the most formative books I've ever read is *The Pursuit of God*, by A.W. Tozer. This book, which Tozer wrote in one night on a train ride from Chicago to Texas, overwhelmed my soul with a deeper understanding of the passion that Christ brought into my life. Tozer described the state of the Church so well:

> The whole transaction of religious conversion has been made mechanical and spiritless… Christ may be "received" without creating any special love for Him in the soul of the receiver. The man is "saved" but he is not hungry nor thirsty after God. In fact, he is specifically taught to be satisfied and is encouraged to be content with little.[9]

And that's just it. The devastation that exists throughout large portions of the Church today, both conservative and liberal, comes from us being taught to be "content with little." This is a travesty and will not invite the power of God to transform our lives and churches. The result is Christianity Lite—tasteless, powerless, Christ-less spirituality. No wonder the world sees the Church as an easily dismissed option.

But God Almighty is not contained in one compartment among many in our lives; He is the reason for our very existence and purpose and deserves to be pursued as such. However, through our pursuit of comfort, material wealth, ease, and self, we have learned the wrong form of contentment. If we are honest, we want life to be easy, we want life to be smooth, and we want life to go our own way without realizing that we often seem to want the "wide road" (Matthew 7:13–14) Jesus warned us about. We so often fail to see that the more we pursue worldly contentment, the more we forfeit the joy we truly seek. In our pursuit of self and ease, we strive for happiness by our own definition. But again, we won't recognize our problem until we believe and see that all true happiness, joy, and fulfillment are found in Christ alone. C.S. Lewis said,

> It would seem that our Lord finds our desires not too strong, but too weak. We are half-hearted creatures, fooling about with drink and sex and ambition when infinite joy is offered us, like an ignorant child who wants to go on making mud pies in a slum because he cannot imagine what is meant by the offer of a holiday at the sea. We are far too easily pleased.[10]

This is precisely why we need a passion for more! More of Him and less of self. The world has crept into the Church and, of course, it's crept into our minds and therefore our hearts. It is blocking our view of the treasure that feeds our zeal. But the Lord, in His love and grace, calls us back to Himself. He calls for our first love (Revelation 2:4). He calls us to see our potential in Him and Him alone.

Very early on, I received from the Lord this mission statement for my life: passionately help people realize their full potential in Jesus Christ. I believe God has placed within me a dissatisfaction with the status quo. I believe God has wired me with an appetite for revival and transformation. I believe God has provoked in me a discontentment for spiritual contentment.

Listen, the reason Jesus Christ has not yet returned is because He's not done building His Church! He obviously has more lives to change, both in salvation and sanctification. He is powerfully at work across this world and He's looking to work powerfully through His Church! As believers, that's you; that's me! Do you believe this?

Let me ask you this question: do you believe God is done changing you? Do you believe that God has reached level six out of ten in your spiritual walk and said, "That's good enough, on to the next person"? Are you kidding? Of course not! God the Father will complete what He started in you by His Son and through His Spirit. So stop long enough to spiritually listen and receive the news that there is so much more that the Lord wants to do in you and me. There is so much more love, so much more joy, so much more faith, so much more life! But with this also comes so much more sacrifice, so much more cost, and so much more death to self. That, too, becomes glorious in the pursuit of passion for more of Christ within us. Oh awesome God, grant us a passion for more of You in us.

## LIFE IN CHRIST IS NOT EASIER, JUST WAY BETTER

I want to make crystal clear that the premise of each of these chapters is an undying and growing passion for Christ, but the result is in no way an easier life. If you truly desire to seek a passion for Christ, you must be willing to die to self. There is simply no other way. I have often said that life in Christ is not easier, just way better.

Frankly, my life before Christ *was* easier, but it was flat-out empty and miserable. Life in Christ is now full of trials, opposition, and a tremendous, heart-wrenching battle against sin. But life is better in Christ! It's precisely within the trials and pain that I continue to discover the joy and grace of the gospel. It's precisely as I die to self (Luke 14:33; John 12:24) that I find my great purpose, plan, and yes, passion for Christ.

If you and I truly want passion for the Lord, we must be willing to take the harder yet supremely better path. Oh Lord, convince us that Your way is right. Convince us that as we die we will truly start to live (Mark 8:35).

This will become your preparation for supernatural passion.

## HELP OUR UNBELIEF

Oh Lord, I pray on behalf of those reading these words that we would start to believe in the passion that could grow within us all. In Jesus' name, may faith start to flow. Forgive us for settling for so little when you desire to do so much. Right now I pray that the husbands and fathers, the wives and mothers, the pastors and leaders, the young adults and singles, and all within our families and churches will believe for so much more. Oh Lord, do so much more!

Unfortunately, this is not the way we usually pray. We knock timidly on God's doorway rather than rattling the gates of heaven with our passion to see God work. How can we ask the Lord for so little when He is the God of all glory?

One of my problems is that I keep reading the Word of God, and within those amazing pages I read about my awesome, unstoppable, and unbreakable God. So you tell me, am I to ask little things from a God who can do all things? No way! How can I not ask great things from a God who can do *all* things? I belong to a God who makes possible the impossible. And all this equates to more faith, to more of His power, and to more passion in and throughout my life. Yes, Lord, revive Your church with passion for more. So much more!

The root of godly passion begins with this: *"Taste and see that the Lord is good."* Because once you've truly tasted Him, nothing else comes close. So this invitation is also a call for faith, a call to believe that there are higher mountains to climb and greater joys to see. Oh it's true, it's so true, if only the Church would begin to believe.

Here is what Charles Spurgeon has to say on this matter:

We ought not to rest content in the mists of the valley when the summit of Tabor awaits us. How pure are the dews of the hills, how fresh is the mountain air, how rich the fare of the dwellers aloft, whose windows look into the New Jerusalem! Many saints are content to live like men in coal mines, who see not the sun. Tears mar their faces when they might anoint them with celestial oil. Satisfied I am that many a believer pines in a dungeon when he might walk on the palace roof, and view the goodly land and Lebanon. *Rouse thee, O believer, from thy low condition! Cast away thy sloth, thy lethargy, thy coldness, or whatever interferes with thy chaste and pure love to Christ. Make Him the source, the center, and the circumference of all thy soul's range of delight. Rest no longer satisfied with thy dwarfish attainments. Aspire to a higher, nobler, a fuller life. Upward to heaven! Nearer to God!* [11]

"Rest no longer in thy dwarfish attainments." Can Spurgeon get an amen from you and me? What would happen if the Church began to believe and actually see the potential we have in Christ?

I pray with great faith that as you read this book, you will start to sense the trickle, and then the flow, of faith into your soul. Sense what the Lord desires to do in you—one life at a time, one family at a time, and one church at a time—and then look out, because here comes the kingdom of Christ!

## CHAPTER THREE
### The Treasure of Passion: The Kingdom

*The kingdom of heaven is like treasure hidden in a field,
which a man found and covered up. Then in his joy he
goes and sells all that he has and buys that field.*
—Matthew 13:44

Come near to the holy men and women of the past and
you will soon feel the heat of their desire after God.[12]
—A.W. Tozer

Do you get the kingdom of heaven? What I really mean is,
do you really grasp the worth of the kingdom of heaven?
The answer can be one of the greatest indicators of our passion
for Jesus Christ, or lack thereof.

Do you understand the worth, the riches, and the treasure
of the kingdom of heaven? Do you truly value what you've
received in Jesus Christ? Do you hold eternal life as your
most precious possession? Do you treasure and marvel at the
gospel and the fact that you are a child of God who has been
granted to share in the riches of the glorious inheritance in
Jesus Christ (Ephesians 1:18)? How we answer these questions

will determine in large part the health of our lives, family, and churches. Do we really *get* the kingdom of heaven?

In ministry, I encounter time and time again believers who intellectually acknowledge that the kingdom of heaven is the great treasure, but they fail to live a life that reflects their belief in that claim. To highlight this contradiction, Jesus told a simple, short, yet life-changing parable:

> *The kingdom of heaven is like treasure hidden in a field, which a man found and covered up. Then in his joy he goes and sells all that he has and buys that field.* (Matthew 13:44)

It was common in Ancient Palestine for people to bury their valuables in the ground. They didn't live in a day like ours with banks, safety deposit boxes, and ATMs, so it makes sense, with the danger of wars, raids, and burglars, that individuals would seek to hide their treasure in a field somewhere outside their homes. Their relatively small houses offered little protection against those who wanted to steal their wealth. The setting of Jesus' story was familiar to His audience.

Sometimes people would bury their treasure, then leave on a journey and, for whatever reason, fail to return. The treasure would be lost and buried. Or others might bury their wealth but kept the location a secret, taking it to the grave. Both these scenarios explain how treasure could easily end up being buried in a field waiting to be discovered.

In the parable, a man stumbles upon a treasure by accident. He understands by law that whoever owns the land also owns whatever is on the land, so *"he goes and sells all that he has and buys that field."* Notice that the man considers this treasure to be so valuable that he will stop at nothing to get it. Nothing.

The text says that he sold "all," everything he had, because the treasure meant so much to him. He had to sell out and forsake all for the sake of the treasure, yet he hadn't bought the treasure itself; it came free with his commitment to buy the land.

Pause a moment and consider this truth: this is what the kingdom of heaven is like. So we ask the life-changing question again. Do we really *get* the kingdom of heaven? The point of this parable is not whether or not we can purchase our salvation—we can't. The point is clearly and profoundly in the worth of the treasure. The priceless treasure starts off as hidden, but when it is found will it be recognized as holding supreme value? God buried the treasure of the gospel right where you would stumble over it; don't walk away from the most precious gift you could ever have! But you'll have to forsake everything else to have it. It's Jesus who said, *"The kingdom of heaven is like treasure…"*

## A CRITICAL SELF-EXAM

We must pause long enough to ask ourselves a question: is the kingdom of heaven our treasure? Is the kingdom of heaven our greatest treasure? Is the kingdom of heaven without question our greatest treasure?

You see, when we understand the kingdom of heaven, we begin to live out the reality that no other treasure even fits in the same category as what God has given us. This is when we prove with our affections, energies, time, and talents that which we truly value, love, and treasure. What is the simplest way to determine what we truly treasure? It's this: how do you spend your thoughts, how do you invest your time, and how do you handle God's money? In other words, examine your thought life, calendar, and bank statements and you will quickly reveal your true treasure.

The power of this simple parable is how profound it becomes as you meditate on it. The reason this man gave up all to get the treasure is that he had figured out that there was no greater value than what he'd just found! At the very moment he discovered the treasure, he failed to care about anything else. In fact, nothing else seemed to hold value or carry the meaning it once did. Notice, too, the delight, job, and hope inherent in this discovery, all because of the value placed on the treasure.

See how quickly the man responded. Notice how readily he decided, and how immediately his life was completely altered by the discovery of the treasure. If we truly get the kingdom of heaven, our lives will start to take on the shape of the kingdom. When you see the worth of the kingdom of heaven and the gospel, everything will change in your value system. Absolutely everything.

The purpose of this chapter is to discover both what fuels and depletes our passion for Christ. This is why Jesus said, *"For where your treasure is, there will your heart be also"* (Luke 12:34). Notice the "where" and "there" in that verse. Find your treasure and then you'll find your heart. It's impossible to separate these two. Your passion and your treasure will always be in the same place. That unavoidable reality is also why Jesus said,

*No servant can serve two masters, for either he will hate the one and love the other, or he will be devoted to the one and despise the other. You cannot serve God and money.* (Luke 16:13)

Why do we try and wiggle out of such concrete truth? We cannot serve two masters. It's not possible. That's why you'll find your heart when you find your treasure.

Another way to examine your life and heart is to ask yourself the following questions.

**Parents:** If I went up to your children and asked them what Mom or Dad loves the most, what would they say? What is your dad most passionate about? Would they answer "his job," "his car," "his sports team," or "his hobby"? Or is there a chance he would say, "He likes other stuff, but for sure my dad loves Jesus Christ the most." Because that's the way it should be.

**Spouses:** If I asked your spouse what your greatest passion is, how would they answer? They know the truth, don't they? They would know what is truly most important in your life and what you truly treasure. They know this because they live with you. They see you behind closed doors and can differentiate between words spoken and a life lived.

**Students:** What treasure are you revealing to your friends? Is it the obsessive need to be accepted by your peers? Is it the clothing you wear? Is it a deep passion for video games? Be honest: what would they say? What would they determine to be your true treasure?

**Retirees:** What treasures are you revealing to those watching you? Are they seeing you very focused on the treasure of the "seen"? Or would they indicate that your true retirement has yet to come within the "unseen" (2 Corinthians 4:17–18)?

**Pastors/leaders:** What treasures are you revealing to your followers? Do those you lead know without question that your true treasure is Jesus Christ and His kingdom? Or would they say that your own ambition, empire, and lust for success is truly your treasure? I recently heard a staff member of another church articulate the fact that he sincerely believes his pastor loves the idea of ministry more than Jesus! Again, find your treasure and find your heart.

Don't you see how essential it is to understand whether or not we truly get the kingdom of heaven? This becomes one of the greatest determining factors in our passion for Christ. Why are so many believers and churches lukewarm? It's because they love their idols more than Jesus Christ.

## ONE THING I DO

Consider now the weight and force of Scripture behind this truth on treasure. We've already mentioned irrefutable passages on truth, but here's one more:

> *But one thing I do: forgetting what lies behind and straining forward to what lies ahead, I press on toward the* goal *for the* prize *of the upward call of God in Christ Jesus.* (Philippians 3:13–14, emphasis added)

Paul starts off this verse with *"But one thing I do…"* That phrase gets my attention due to the simplicity and profundity of what's about to be said. You could use it as a definition of passion: *"But one thing I do…"*

He then goes on to say that whatever is the past is the past, and now he's straining, putting all his energy into what actually matters and is essential. Notice that he presses on to the goal. But what's the goal? It's the *"prize of the upward call."* And what's the "prize"? Aha! It's the treasure of Jesus Christ! So, the whole motivation, purpose, and goal of Paul's life revolves around his single-minded pursuit of the gospel, the treasure of the kingdom of heaven. This truth allows him to see the rest of the world as having no value when compared to the surpassing worth of knowing Christ (Philippians 3:8). Examine the words of J.C. Ryle on this life-changing theme:

> A zealous person in Christianity is preeminently a person of one thing… They have a passion for one thing, and that one thing is to please God and to

advance God's glory. If they are consumed in the very burning of their passion for God, they don't care—they are content. They feel that, like a candle, they were made to burn; and if they are consumed in the burning, then they have only done the work for which God has appointed them. Such a person will always find a sphere for their zeal.[13]

Oh how I love the one thing I do. Can you see the simplicity in this verse, along with the simplicity of the parable in Matthew 13? There's such a singlemindedness, such undivided devotion, and such a distraction-free life. And it's all because of the worth, value, and understood price of what's been found and given in the gospel. Awesome!

Don't you see then where passion comes from? Passion is not an overhyped, fanatical display of emotion. No, true passion is a natural and necessary response to the greatest gift ever given in Jesus Christ. If you know what you've been given, you will "sell all" to make your entire life about this treasure.

### TREASURE ▶ JOY ▶ SACRIFICE

These three things—treasure, joy, and sacrifice—all occur within Matthew 13:44:

> *The kingdom of heaven is like treasure hidden in a field, which a man found and covered up. Then in his joy he goes and sells all that he has and buys that field.*

It thrills me to show you this truth. As soon as the treasure is found and properly valued, joy is the immediate result. However, the power doesn't end with the joy; the joy causes him to go and sacrifice *"all that he has,"* and then he buys the field.

That sequence fires me up! There's no hesitation, groaning, or burden associated with this sacrifice. That's because it's a sacrifice of joy placed within the value of the treasure. He knows he's got the deal of a lifetime! Wow! The gospel is amazingly powerful when it's truly ascertained and then applied. Please, Lord, help us to see and live this.

So often when we ask our kids to do a simple task they don't want to do, it becomes such an ordeal, with whining over how great a sacrifice they're making. We hear sighs and groans of "Do I *have* to, Dad?" or "When will I be done, Dad?" or "I'm so tired and exhausted, Dad!"

We, as children of God, can approach the work and privilege of the kingdom in similar ways: "Do I have to, God? Isn't there someone else? But God, I'm so tired and I don't feel like it!" Can you see that whining to God about our "sacrifice" is really a heart and vision problem? The moment we feel it's a great burden to serve and sacrifice for the Lord, our alarm bells should go off; our value system is messed up, and therefore our joy is diminished and our attitude suffering greatly. If we fail to see the true treasure, then fatigue, complacency, and apathy come rushing in. We lose sight of the gospel and lose our zeal. This is a significant transition, for if we truly see the treasure of the kingdom, joy fills our hearts and joyful sacrifice fills our lives. This doesn't mean that we won't struggle from time to time and have setbacks, but it does mean that we'll know that our eyes need to be on the prize, intentionally "forgetting" what lies behind.

## THE SOURCE OF URGENCY

Can you see now how we can live with more passion and therefore with more urgency? Even as I write this, I feel urgency growing within me because of my passion for the kingdom of heaven. It's the truth of God's Word renewing my mind for the glory of God. Imagine that! Where there's true passion, there's true urgency.

Think of a child on Christmas morning and the urgency that fills her to discover presents under the tree. Why the rushing down the stairs, the jumping up and down in place, and bright eyes and eager expectation? Why is it she doesn't wake up on school days with the same urgency and anticipation? It's because passion drives her.

Why is it that so many men wake up in the dark and leap out of bed with joy to play golf, fired up to hit the course at the break of dawn? Yet the same man will be a sloth in his attempt to wake up and spend time with the Lord at the same hour. Why do so many people line up for hours on Black Friday or Boxing Day (Canada) and wait in the freezing cold just to purchase their next gadget or flat-screen TV? Yet the same people stroll into church late every single weekend. Why is that? It's because our passion drives us. What we are passionate about determines what we make sacrifices for, and this is why apathy is killing the Church. It's ultimately a heart issue.

My goal is not to load you with guilt, but to fill you with conviction from the Holy Spirit. I long to help you see that when you truly treasure the kingdom of heaven and the gospel, everything in your life will begin to change. Remember: there won't be a nagging, irritating voice trying to ruin your life. No way! What you hear will be the voice of the Holy Spirit inviting you to true life, true joy, and yes, true passion! A passion fuelled by the grace of the gospel.

## MOTIVATED BY THE REWARD

I want to share one more verse on the connection between passion, joy, and cost. Again, look for the sequence of the treasure, the joy, and the sacrifice: *"He (Moses) considered the reproach of Christ greater wealth than the treasures of Egypt, for he was looking to the reward"* (Hebrews 11:26).

Moses viewed the disgrace and suffering of Christ to be of greater wealth than all the treasure of Egypt? Really? How is that possible? It's possible because of how the verse ends: *"for he was looking to the reward."* There it is again: the reward is the treasure, and when the treasure is clearly seen, not even all the treasure in Egypt will compare with what is found in the gospel and glory of Jesus Christ.

If we go back to our original parable in Matthew 13, we will see that the economic transaction represents a spiritual transaction involving the surrender of our lives. The moment we correctly value our treasure in Christ, we will be able to let go of all, if necessary, for the sake of the kingdom.

In recent days, reports from around this world have been telling of Christians who face execution yet will not recant their faith in Jesus Christ. People fed on a constant diet that devalues faith sit back in amazement. Why would anyone accept death rather than deny Christ? The world doesn't get it. True followers of Jesus won't forsake Him because there's nothing else worth living for. When you've already received the greatest treasure there is, why would you settle for anything less?

Today, as throughout history, believers are being asked to deny Jesus Christ with a knife to their throats, and their refusal results in giving up their lives on earth to be with their Saviour in heaven. That is the natural outworking of a passion that is truly rooted in the kingdom of heaven and the gospel of Jesus Christ. That is why Paul said, *"For to me to live is Christ, and to die is gain"* (Philippians 1:21). Amen.

## PURSUING A PASSION FOR THE KINGDOM

At this point, you may be thinking, *What do words like "getting it," "selling everything," and "treasure" have to do with my understanding of Jesus? How do I grow a true passion for the kingdom of heaven and the gospel?* Consider what would make you ask these questions or feel this conviction. What was it that turned your heart and desire towards Christ and His treasure? The answer to that question is the answer to the earlier questions. You've just tripped over the treasure; what are you going to do next?

I often witness moments like this when preaching to our wonderful church. I see the power of God's Spirit move among the congregation with conviction. I then point out what should be obvious: whatever has driven this conviction, repentance, and renewed desire is what you need to take with you each and every day.

This chapter primarily highlighted truth from God's Word and applied it to your heart. Your mind has been engaged, and therefore your affections for Christ have been stirred. Even as I write these words my attention is sharp, my convictions strong, my mind renewed, and my passion heating up. Why? Because what we are thinking about is true! I know my true treasure, and therefore I want to guard it, share it, and enjoy it with my whole being.

The patterns of life that flow from rightly valuing the kingdom of heaven must be lived out each and every day. Trust me; I need this *each and every day*. I need to expose my mind and heart to the true treasure so that I can destroy the lies of the false treasures that seek to seep into my mind, affections, and will.

So I ask: how ready are you to pursue a passion for the kingdom? The rest of this book lays out the patterns found in God's Word that add up to a life sold out for the kingdom of God.

- Repent of any and all false treasures (Chapter Four).
- Focus on your reward (Chapter Five).
- Live for what God blesses (Chapter Six).
- Renew your mind (Chapter Seven).
- Pray for such passion (Chapter Eight).
- Simplify your life (Chapter Nine).
- Anticipate God's move (Chapter Ten and Eleven).

Do you see how passion for the Lord is weaved together through all the disciplines and truths of the Christian life? The fire of passion is being stoked; let's throw on some more logs.

### FURTHER THOUGHT AND REFLECTION

- Where are you on the sequence of treasure  joy  sacrifice? How long has it been since you've seen the real treasure?
- What do your thoughts, time, and wallet truly reveal? Be honest. Do you have a pursuit and passion for the kingdom or something else?
- My friend Daniel Henderson uses the phrase "weapons of mass distraction." Where and what is distracting you from singlemindedness of the treasure of the kingdom?
- Read and meditate on Matthew 13:44–45, Philippians 3:13–14, and Hebrews 11:24–26. Meditation means making every word count. Take some time to allow each word to move your heart towards passion for Christ.

## CHAPTER FOUR
### The Beauty of Passion: Brokenness

*The Lord is near to the brokenhearted and saves the crushed in spirit.*

—Psalm 34:18

I am sure that whatever God may despise… He will not despise the broken and contrite heart.[14]

—Charles Simeon

Understand, as we talk about and urge true passion for Christ, that this is not something we can contrive on our own. True passion will be born out of ashes, rising from the devastation of self, and what the Bible calls the crucifixion of self (Galatians 2:20) only comes through true brokenness.

Acknowledging our condition before God is an essential step in understanding passion, because true passion cannot be self-generated or faked. Our spiritual bankruptcy, or poverty of spirit, is why biblical brokenness is absolutely necessary. Because authentic brokenness results in true passion, there are no exceptions to this biblical truth. The route to passion always leads through the valley of brokenness.

Biblical brokenness is beautiful—maybe not to the world or your neighbour, but it's beautiful to Jesus. I believe the Bible teaches that our brokenness is irresistible to God. It's irresistible to Him because it's so beautiful to Him.

Brokenness is a demonstration and combination of humility, dependence, desperation, surrender, and true, unadulterated worship. We must be shattered by recognizing that we have nothing God needs, and yet He loves and wants *us*. Brokenness cannot be faked because it's not of us, it's of God. And it is beautiful and powerful. Within true brokenness, pride is forgotten, self is ignored, and grace is breathed in like fresh air.

## A PICTURE OF BROKENNESS

One of my favourite passages of Scripture, which just happens to be one of the most beautiful pictures of brokenness, is found in Luke 7. This is the story of the sinful woman Luke describes as *"a woman of the city, who was a sinner"* (Luke 7:37). This is God's Word letting us know both her practice of sin and reputation for sin.

The passage also reveals to us that Jesus was invited to a Pharisee's house to eat with him. As the meal was served in this context of tremendous external righteousness (a Pharisee's house), the sinful woman learned of Jesus' presence, and in spite of her obvious external unrighteousness she decided to express love. The sinful woman arrived at the house with a flask of alabaster ointment and did the unthinkable: she stood behind Jesus, wept, wet His feet, and wiped her tears off them with her very own hair. She then kissed His feet and anointed them with the ointment. What a moment this must have been, what a display of love, of affection, of humble brokenness. She performed an unexpected and stunningly beautiful gesture.

Jesus, of course, would use this very example to point out to Simon the Pharisee the power and response of true grace and true brokenness. He knew how badly Simon misread the woman's actions, so Jesus told the parable of two debtors, of whom *"[o]ne owned five hundred denarii, and the other fifty"* (Luke 7:41). Both debts were cancelled by the moneylender. Jesus then turned to Simon and asked, *"Now which of them will love him more?"* (Luke 7:42) The Bible goes on to say:

> *Simon answered, "The one, I suppose, for whom he cancelled the larger debt."*
>
> *And [Jesus] said to him, "You have judged rightly." Then turning toward the woman he said to Simon, "Do you see this woman? I entered your house; you gave me no water for my feet, but she has wet my feet with her tears and wiped them with her hair. You gave me no kiss, but from the time I came in she has not ceased to kiss my feet. You did not anoint my head with oil, but she has anointed my feet with ointment. Therefore I tell you, her sins, which are many, are forgiven—for she loved much. But he who is forgiven little, loves little."* (Luke 7:43–47)

The whole point of this remarkable interaction, according to Jesus, is that the more you are aware of the grace that has been extended to you in Christ, the more you will manifest the fruit of love and brokenness in your life.

The word brokenness may not be used in this text, but it is demonstrated without a doubt. Consider the factors of true brokenness seen in the life of the sinful woman:

- Her total disregard for the fear of man, and for the fear of God. (She enters the house of a Pharisee and loves on Jesus).

- Her incredible display of humility. (She wept, washed, and wiped the feet of Jesus.)
- Her wonderful, unashamed display of affection. (She kissed Jesus' feet, full of emotion.)
- Her zero signs of pride, and many signs of love. (She showed no hesitation when she poured out the ointment.)
- Her proper and right emotional response. (She was completely overwhelmed by grace.)
- She was fully aware of her undeserved grace, and fully aware of the deity of Christ. (She had been forgiven much, and loved much.)
- Her gratitude, adoration, and worship. (She continually wept and kissed Jesus' feet.)

All of these are found in this passage, and all are the fruit of brokenness. Consider as well how much this meant to our Saviour. He honoured, drew attention to, and made her an example of what matters most, letting this woman know how much God loved her, perhaps for the first time in her life.

In a different event with similar themes, the gospels tell the story of another woman who anointed Jesus. This time, the location was Simon the leper's house (not to be confused with Simon the Pharisee). When the woman anointed the head of Jesus with very expensive balm, onlookers were indignant over the apparent waste of the ointment. They even went to the extent of scolding the woman. Jesus, however, would have none of it. He said,

*Why do you trouble her? She has done a beautiful thing to me. For you always have the poor with you, and whenever you want, you can do good for them. But you will not always have me. She has done what she could;*

*she has anointed my body beforehand for burial.* (Mark 14:6–8).

Then Jesus added this amazing note: *"And truly, I say to you, wherever the gospel is proclaimed in the whole world, what she has done will be told in memory of her"* (Mark 14:9). Consider the magnitude of this statement. The act was so significant and beautiful to Jesus that He promised it would be told wherever the gospel was proclaimed, in memory of her. Now, His words are not to be taken lightly or casually glossed over. That is a statement of massive significance in understanding what Jesus treasures, values, and looks for in His followers. In a word: He looks for brokenness.

This is the reason that in one of the hardest moments of King David's life, he called out, *"The sacrifices of God are a broken spirit; a broken and contrite heart, O God, you will not despise"* (Psalm 51:17). So please receive this truth: if pride is God-repellent (James 4:6), then brokenness is God-attractant. Again, as David says, *"a broken and contrite heart, O God, you will not despise."*

## PRIDE IS STUPID

Do you agree that pride is stupid? If you read your Bible, you should. Understanding the stupidity of pride is good theology that seems too often overlooked.

Consider in Scripture how often the Lord refers to the disaster of pride in the hearts of His people. Over and over again it's the accusation against stubborn hearts, stiff-necked people who refuse to listen, and lovers of evil. Repeatedly the Lord reaches out to His people who are not broken but seem rather put together on their own plan and agenda, pursuing their own desires. And every single time, in their own pride, they lose.

That's why pride is so idiotic, because with pride you can never truly win. Never. You feel like you're going to win, you convince yourself that pride wins, you believe the deceitfulness of your own heart, but in the end pride always loses.

Consider the impact of pride upon our hearts. Stop long enough to recognize the fruit of pride within us. When we are stubborn in our own ways, we demonstrate that we are self-righteous. When we are stiff-necked, we reveal we are trying to be self-sufficient. When we are lovers of idols and evil, we prove that we are little self-worshippers. This frame of mind is scary, but it shows the futility and stupidity of pride. We become convinced of things that are absolutely ridiculous and preposterous.

Pride produces a heart that cannot be moulded, a heart that is hard and resistant to change. Pride produces a heart that feels like it's in total control, possessing all knowledge and needing nothing. How ridiculous pride is. I have often marvelled at the Pharisee in Luke 18:11 as he openly condemned and insulted the tax collector off in the corner. In his pride-filled blindness, he exclaimed, *"God, I thank you that I am not like other men… or even like this tax collector."* The astounding insight of this moment is that the man the Pharisee was condemning was the very man God actually wanted him to be like! But because he was so blind, though he was thanking God that he was not the tax collector, in reality he was far worse. Oh how poisonous pride is in our lives. It makes us dumb.

But if those are the shameful symptoms of pride, consider the beauty of brokenness. Rather than being put together, brokenness understands that it's fractured, inadequate, insufficient, and in tremendous need of any and all grace. Brokenness shamelessly calls out for rescue, wisdom, strength, and forgiveness. In short, while brokenness calls out for grace, pride needs no grace. This is why success has destroyed a man over and over again, while so often failure makes the man. Success is the greatest temptation of pride while failure becomes an opportunity to recognize our true and great need for someone beyond ourselves.

A little while ago, while in Philadelphia I had the opportunity to visit the National Historic Park where the Liberty Bell and Independence Hall are located. I was also able to see portions of the Declaration of Independence. One of the founders' quotes put up for display came from the New Hampshire Convention from 1781, and it said, "The love of Power is so alluring that few have ever been able to resist its bewitching influence." This piece of wisdom was part of the very fabric that undergirded the founding of the United States.

Two hundred and fifty years later, are we any different? If the founding fathers of a nation believed this, should not we be ever more careful over our hearts' propensity towards sinful pride? Yet we regularly see how success and power fuel pride, and pride becomes the downfall and destruction of so many who once started with good intentions.

As James 4:6 says, *"God opposes the proud, but gives grace to the humble."* And 1 Peter 5:5 says, *"Clothe yourselves, all of you, with humility toward one another, for 'God opposes the proud but gives grace to the humble.'"* You certainly don't have to be a biblical scholar to understand the impact of pride versus humility. With pride you lose, and with humility and brokenness you win. No wonder the very next verse in 1 Peter 5:6 says, *"Humble yourselves, therefore…"* Of course that's the next command, because who could be dumb enough to think pride is a good idea? Convince yourself that *pride is dumb*. Literally preach to yourself that you will lose with pride every time. Remind yourself forcefully that God rushes to the aid of the broken and contrite heart. Persuade yourself of the biblical truth that every time you choose the door of pride, you choose defeat, but every time you choose the door of brokenness and humility, you choose to win by the grace of God.

This is why we must have a passion for brokenness. It is the condition in which God works and the circumstances in which He moves. The heart of true brokenness is irresistible to God (Psalm 51:7; Isaiah 57:15). However, fake brokenness tells another story.

## FAKE BROKENNESS

Mark 7 reveals to us how God views a lack of true brokenness. Jesus Himself condemns the Pharisees and quotes Isaiah: *"This people honors me with their lips, but their heart is far from me; in vain do they worship me…"* (Mark 7:6–7) Now notice what Jesus is saying: there is an appearance of godliness, devotion, and brokenness, but in reality it's a superficial show. The Pharisees can speak the right language, but their hearts are far from the One they profess to serve. That is incredible.

The Pharisees contained so much truth in the mind, yet it hadn't affected their hearts. They believed they were close to the One they claimed to follow, yet they couldn't be further away. They stood talking face to face with the Son of God Himself, yet they didn't know it. What were they missing? Brokenness!

In this very verse, it's pride that pushed them away from the Lord, that hardened their hearts. However, inherent in the verse is also the reality of brokenness, tenderness, humility, and affection. All these things draw us near to the Lord. Instead of being "far from him," we would be oh so near to Him. This is exactly why we must have a continual desire for and conviction of brokenness in our lives. It is the soil from which all true fruit grows. You and I cannot, and will not, see a true passion for Christ within our lives if we reject the soil of brokenness.

## THE SOIL OF BROKENNESS

A. W. Tozer has so aptly stated, "It is doubtful whether God can bless a man greatly until he has hurt him deeply."[15] God the Father understands the beauty of brokenness, so He allows trials to enter our lives to produce it. He loves us too much to let us carry on alone. He loves us too much to see us to pursue our own selfish desires and ambitions. He cares for us too much to simply let us be destroyed by our pride-filled idolatry and heart-numbing materialism. He loves us too much to see us wander away into fruitless oblivion. So He allows trials to come, so that brokenness may be cultivated. It is an incredible act of grace and love upon our lives, and through trials we grow in wisdom as we see why and how God works.

Consider the truth that every single person in the Bible who was powerfully used of God was tested and wounded deeply in some way. Every single person. Consider that every believer over the course of Church history who has been powerfully used has also been painfully broken. I haven't found an exception. So tell me, are you and I then supposed to expect something different? Are you and I going to be the first people ever in the history of the world to be powerfully used for Christ without being broken? I don't think so, and neither should you.

The words of Hosea 10:12 are representative of everything I've been saying: *"Sow for yourselves righteousness; reap steadfast love; break up your fallow ground, for it is time to seek the Lord, that he may come and rain righteousness upon you."* Is that not a beautiful verse? Notice the action words sow, reap, break up, and seek, which lead to *"that he may come."* That's the power of brokenness. It places a huge sign above our lives that says,

"Sow the fruit of the Spirit here." The necessity of brokenness is a painful, wonderful, glorious, and beautiful reality. It is also why our "most powerful adoration of God will grow best in the ploughed soil of our contrition."[16]

## CONSISTENT DOSES OF HUMILIATION

I have often said that consistent doses of humiliation are among the greatest gifts God has granted to me in my life and ministry. Those who know me best can attest to these embarrassments and the benefits that have flowed from them.

It never ceases to amaze me how creative the Lord can be in drumming up humiliation in my life. Some of it is obvious, but most is only seen between the Lord and me. Over the years, as much as it hurts, the stumbles and weaknesses have been a constant source of blessing, and yes, further humiliation.

These humiliating experiences are varied and vast. I remember when I was a fairly new Christian with increasing opportunities to preach. I had confidence in Christ, but I also had a confidence in self that needed to be identified and crushed.

On one occasion, I was invited to preach at a university campus, and was thrilled to discover that the room was packed and the anticipation great. In my immaturity and arrogance, I believed that I had something to say, and God would use me. However, less than halfway through my meagre message, out of nowhere I took on a dry mouth that I had never experienced before. I'm not exaggerating when I say that I could barely get my mouth open. The memory still stirs up vivid emotions of complete helplessness. It became so painfully obvious how bad I was struggling that I could sense the mood in the room become awkward; the audience became embarrassed and concerned for me. Someone handed me a bottle of water and I suffered through the remainder of the message. Needless to say, I was not invited back.

Though I had never experienced dry mouth before that event, I struggled with the problem for years after. Why? I can't say for sure, but it resulted in a humbling dependence upon the Lord every single time I spoke. From then on, I took nothing for granted. My awareness of my need for the Lord and His Spirit increased a hundredfold. I was not in danger of overconfidence anymore; I was trying to muster the faith to speak at all. I didn't see other people struggle with this problem. It was a special grace of humiliation just for me. And it worked!

The time came when the dry mouth stopped. I don't struggle with it now, but why did it happen then? At its root, I fundamentally believe it was the Lord humiliating me in His grace in order to save me from myself.

Many other times, the Lord has allowed a severe season of testing in a relationship in my life, or permitted significant spiritual opposition that literally brought me to my knees with tears and brokenness. This is exactly what the Lord used to keep Paul from being "too elated," by allowing "a messenger of Satan" to torment him (2 Corinthians 12:7–8). And why did the Lord do this? To keep Paul's attention on the sufficiency of God's grace. In these moments, Paul's weakness became God's strength. God decidedly broke His servant. He humbled Paul in order to use him. You and I are no different.

Can you stop right now and thank the Lord for times of humiliation? It's a powerful place to be when you learn to squeeze the blessing of grace from the difficulties and stunning setbacks of life—even the ones that are clearly your own fault.

Trust me, I don't enjoy the times of shame. In fact, all the pride within me wants to escape exposure. But after the waves of embarrassment settle down and I find myself broken, humbled, and in awe of the gospel, I give thanks and praise to my wondrous and gracious Saviour. I am convinced that I would not be in ministry today if it were not for the gracious acts of God's humiliation in my life. The medicine of humiliation becomes the antidote to the poison of my pride. This is because shame, stumbling, and weakness cause me to run to the grace of the gospel.

The amazing grace of the gospel is the true antidote to pride. In my humiliation, I go from being the self-righteous Pharisee in Luke 18 to the beat-up tax collector in the corner, saying, *"God, be merciful to me, a sinner!"* (Luke 18:13) Oh the grace and love that is found within our humiliation. Are you able to agree with that statement? Only pride would hold you back.

## HUMBLE YET STRONG

Allow me clear up some misconceptions regarding brokenness and humility. Humility is not weak, but rather true strength. Humility is the path to greatness, and it was both taught and exemplified by the Lord Jesus Christ.

I love the realization that came to me as I was studying John 13, visualizing Jesus washing His disciples' feet. Here was the Lord Himself, modelling one of the most important lessons He would ever give on leadership, humility, and love. With bowl and towel, Jesus lowered Himself to take on the role of a servant by performing a task so humble that it brought embarrassment to His own disciples. Peter, of course, fought against the idea of Jesus doing this to him, and then, seemingly exasperated, said, *"You shall never wash my feet"* (John 13:8). The act of humility was so humiliating to Peter that he couldn't take it. But Jesus responded, *"If I do not wash you, you have no share with me"* (John 13:8).

Here's the point I want you to see and never forget. As Jesus was powerfully humbling Himself before His disciples, notice that no one questioned who was in charge. Do you see that? I love the truth of humble strength so much that I want to write it again: as *Jesus washed His disciples' feet, no one questioned who was in charge.* The act of Jesus' humility did not lessen His strength or authority, but rather increased it.

That's a lesson few believe deeply enough to practice. So many leaders seek to control and demand service. Leadership today is about power, perks, prestige, and position. Jesus' example is to serve, but serve with strength. In Him, we find humble strength. Oh how beautiful humility is and how strong humility can be. It becomes a brokenness in self, yet a Holy Spirit effusion from God. Amen! Pursue true brokenness and you will find true strength.

## THE POWER OF CULTIVATION

When I was a university student, I worked for a couple of seasons as a landscaper. One of the things I quickly grew to appreciate is the power of cultivation. The opportunity to cultivate the soil was exciting, but this is because hard soil stifled growth. It was compacted and cracked. It not only looked bad, it felt bad. However, if you were to grab a cultivator and start to break up the ground, the soil would change so much, becoming soft, workable, prepared, and fertile. I loved cultivating soil—both dirt and human!

I think one of the reasons I love cultivating the hard ground and seeing it become broken and productive is because it's a metaphor for what I desperately want in my own life. I hate it when I have a hard heart, when I have an attitude that's unresponsive and lacking affection. I can't stand my heart when it feels dry and cracked and difficult for the Spirit of God to move in. But this is when a fresh experience of brokenness becomes the very thing I need. This is when the Lord comes and rains righteousness down upon me, revitalizing my heart and life. When I'm being ploughed and furrowed, worship springs forth and confession comes easily. This is when the fruit of passion is most clearly seen.

Loved ones, pursue with passion the power of brokenness in your life. When you are broken by God, you better understand the gospel and your need for Christ—and that produces an unrelenting zeal for God. There is nothing quite like it. Always remember, *"The Lord is near to the brokenhearted and saves the crushed in spirit"* (Psalm 34:18).

## FURTHER THOUGHT AND REFLECTION

- In what areas of your life right now might God be trying to cultivate the soil of brokenness? Are you resisting in pride?
- It's amazing to me how many believers fear the reality of being broken. Our pride fears losing control. Where, by faith, can you invite brokenness right now?
- When was the last time you had an experience like that of the sinful woman in Luke 7? Recently? Never? Beg God for the grace to see the glory and beauty of God through your own soil of brokenness.
- Study right now Daniel 4:28–37 and Luke 5:5–11. What themes of humiliation, brokenness, and grace do you see?

## CHAPTER FIVE
The Pursuit of Passion: Eternity

*But our citizenship is in heaven, and from it we await a Savior, the Lord Jesus Christ...*

—Philippians 3:20

If I find in myself a desire which no experience in this world can satisfy, the most probable explanation is that I was made for another world.[17]

—C.S. Lewis

It has been said that those who are heavenly minded are of no earthly good. I don't think I could disagree more. Heavenly mindedness is an aspect of the Christian life that brings true identity to the soul. I am resolved in my thinking that those who consider most the reality of their heavenly future will have the greatest impact upon the world in the present. It is the compelling call of heaven that frees us from the whispered idolatry of the world, it is the anticipation of heaven that allows us to see today with true eternal vision, and it is the reality of heaven that causes us to live out our true identity and citizenship.

## MY CITIZENSHIP IS HEAVENESE

The apostle Paul said in Philippians 3:20, *"But our citizenship is in heaven…"* This was stated in contrast to the enemies of the Christian faith, the lovers of this world whose *"god is their belly, and they glory in their shame, with minds set on earthly things"* (Philippians 3:19). But a child of God's view on life is oh so different and oh so glorious. Our identity is not found in this world; our identity is found with Christ, and therefore with Him in heaven.

Now, I am all for national pride. I was born in raised in Canada and I am very thankful for my country. I am blessed to currently live in such freedom and to experience such common grace. I value the rich history of Canada and the ideals that it was founded upon. I don't take for granted the laws of this land and the rich resources that are provided for all citizens who live under the maple leaf flag. I enjoy the four distinct seasons and I certainly well up with pride, and occasionally teary eyes, as Canada secures yet another Olympic hockey gold medal.

Having stated that, here's what I know to be spiritually true: when it comes down to it, I am not merely Canadian; in a deeper reality I am Heavenese. At the moment of my conversion, my soul was reborn and I was granted new spiritual life in Him. My flesh was put to death and my inheritance of glory guaranteed. I became a child of God, an adopted member of God's family. I became Heavenese. This is my spiritual reality, and if you are truly saved in Jesus Christ, this is your spiritual reality, too. The point is, let's live like it! Consider these verses, which reinforce this truth:

> *But our citizenship is in heaven, and from it we await a Savior, the Lord Jesus Christ, who will transform our lowly body to be like his glorious body, by the power that enables*

*him even to subject all things to himself.* (Philippians 3:20–21)

*He has delivered us from the domain of darkness and transferred us to the kingdom of his beloved Son, in whom we have redemption, the forgiveness of sins.* (Colossians 1:13–14)

*For here we have no lasting city, but we seek the city that is to come.* (Hebrews 13:14)

*In my Father's house are many rooms. If it were not so, would I have told you that I go to prepare a place for you?* (John 14:2).

*…to an inheritance that is imperishable, undefiled, and unfading, kept in heaven for you…* (1 Peter 1:4)

*And I saw the holy city, new Jerusalem, coming down out of heaven from God, prepared as a bride adorned for her husband.* (Revelation 21:2)

*But as it is, they desire a better country, that is, a heavenly one.* (Hebrews 11:16)

*But according to his promise we are waiting for new heavens and a new earth in which righteousness dwells.* (2 Peter 3:13)

The truth is that we were made for more, and in Christ and because of Christ this "more" is on its way. This then becomes both our destination and our identity. It is right and biblical to allow our citizenship in heaven to drive our ambition and motivations here on earth. When we lose this, we lose our focus, direction, and passion.

## ETERNITY AMNESIA

I have heard Paul Tripp use the term "identity amnesia," and I love it. It's helpful to see that when we suffer from identity amnesia, the problem will certainly lead to eternity amnesia. After all, Ecclesiastes 3:11 says that God *"has put eternity into man's heart."* We are hardwired with an eternal connection that longs to be completed. Our identity in Jesus Christ plugs us into eternity and allows us to live for more than what we see. This truth frees us from being enslaved by the temporal happiness and temporary trials of this world. 2 Corinthians 4:16–17 says it so well:

> *So we do not lose heart. Though our outer self is wasting away, our inner self is being renewed day by day. For this light momentary affliction is preparing for us an eternal weight of glory beyond all comparison...*

The lifestyle the apostle Paul is describing is so good and so true. The reality of our identity, and therefore eternity, allows us to wholeheartedly say and believe that *"this light momentary affliction"* is just part of our journey to heaven.

Who else can boast of such an outlook other than a child of God and believer in Jesus Christ? This is our truth and reality each and every day. Our physical trials, emotional sorrows, relational struggles, and yes, spiritual difficulties are all preparing us for what will be *"an eternal weight of glory beyond all comparison."* Hallelujah! Praise the Lord! This is the power of truth that liberates us from the bondage of the present world and frees us to seek the reality of heaven. In other words, astra petamus…

## ASTRA PETAMUS

One of my spiritual heroes is George Whitefield, a man who exemplifies all that I've been stating thus far. He decided that he loved Jesus, was called by Jesus, and then lived all-out for Jesus in every possible way. If you want to be blessed with great inspiration and moved towards spiritual passion, I strongly recommend Arnold Dallimore's biography of Whitefield.[18]

During the eighteenth century, it was quite common for men to have a crest with which to emboss the wax they used to seal their letters. These personal symbols would often carry a short motto. The motto of George Whitefield's seal was "Astra Petamus," which in Latin means "Let us seek heaven."[19] Awesome!

Here's how Iain Murray described the passion and the secret to Whitefield's life:

> He was profoundly influenced by the consciousness of the brevity of this present pilgrimage. Only the narrow stream of death separates every generation of Christians from the church in glory.[20]

Murray tells us that Whitefield was "profoundly influenced by the consciousness of the brevity of this present pilgrimage." John Wesley had this to say of Whitefield:

> Have we read or heard of any person since the Apostles, who testified the gospel of the grace of God through so widely extended a space, through so large a part of the inhabited world? Above all, have we read or heard of any, who has been a blessed instrument in his hand of

bringing so many sinners from "darkness to light, and from the power of Satan unto God?"[21]

When we stop and think of the society-changing fruit of a man like George Whitefield, can we identify the reason for such impact? Well, we know his effectiveness was under the sovereignty of God, but we also know that God's Word clearly tells us over and over again that we have a choice of whether to be used by the Lord. I argue that it's because Whitefield was so aware and conscious of how short this life really was that he decided to go all in for the gospel of Jesus Christ. He saw heaven each day approaching with greater speed and he let that urgency affect the way he lived.

James asks us, *"What is your life? For you are a mist that appears for a little time and then vanishes"* (James 4:14). But life's brevity didn't discourage Whitefield; it thoroughly motivated him to pursue his reality and preach his heart out with the gospel that others might know this same altered view of life. Oh that we would be called to the same! Oh that our passion for heaven would start to impact our present actions.

We must realize that our life is a pinprick on a line of eternity that extends from Vancouver to Halifax (or Los Angeles to New York). Even that comparison is insufficient. The point is that when you realize how short this life really is, and that you've been given only one crack at this, it's time to get serious. When you face the reality that the return of the Lord is imminent and that you will soon be presented to Christ in glory, something shifts in you. When you accept that this place called earth is not your true home, your values change. The following shifts in priority happen:

• You care less for matters on earth.

- You care more for people on earth.
- You spend less time collecting the things of earth.
- You spend more time collecting people for heaven.
- You less often find fulfillment in the temporal.
- You more often find true joy and satisfaction in the eternal.
- Your stress decreases in the present
- Your prayers increase for the future.

This is just a sampling of the impact of your passion being rooted in the eternal. The fruit is truly unending.

## IT'S GOOD TO GROAN

The Scriptures that point us in this direction are overwhelming and glorious. One of my favourites is found in Romans 8:18–24:

> *For I consider that the sufferings of this present time are not worth comparing with the glory that is to be revealed to us. For the creation waits with eager longing for the revealing of the sons of God. For the creation was subjected to futility, not willingly, but because of him who subjected it, in hope that the creation itself will be set free from its bondage to corruption and obtain the freedom of the glory of the children of God. For we know that the whole creation has been groaning together in the pains of childbirth until now. And not only the creation, but we ourselves, who have the firstfruits of the Spirit, groan inwardly as we wait eagerly for adoption as sons, the redemption of our bodies. For in this hope we were saved.*

I have to admit, my eyes light up and my heart beats faster as I read this: *"but we ourselves… groan inwardly as we wait eagerly for adoption as sons, the redemption of our bodies. For in this hope we were saved."* You see, we are not only given permission to groan physically, we are also expected to groan in our spiritual lives. The moment we were saved in Jesus Christ, we were born again to a new life that will be perfectly fulfilled through glorification.

The text says that this is our hope of our salvation. No wonder then that the closer we find ourselves to the beauty and glory of Jesus Christ, the more we begin to groan. No wonder our frail bodies, which are breaking down, creaking, and often hurting, can actually feel the distance from perfection. I find myself waking up with new injuries all the time! Why? Because our outward-wasting bodies (2 Corinthians 4:16) are calling out for something so much greater. No wonder we cry over sin and feel such deep pain as the evil of our day rips through life after life. We are groaning for our future reality, that we might see our Saviour face to face (1 Corinthians 13).

Let me say it again: it's good to groan. As we groan, we are constantly reminded of what is true and what is not, instead of trying to lie to ourselves in desperate attempts to defy aging and wrap up all our security in how we look or what we own. Here we see that death is inevitable, but in reality life awaits!

The text also refers to *"we... who have the first fruits of the Spirit."* Just as Christ was raised from the dead to an imperishable and indestructible body, we too are promised this in our life in Christ. So what does this understanding do? It directs our minds to truth that transforms, moves our affections to the One who saves, and urges our wills toward the destination of heaven. But again, this does not make us useless for the present. I believe that heaven's perspective, when rightly applied, makes us all the more potent with the gospel... right now.

I pray that you are starting to see more and more where true passion lies. When you believe that what you're reading is God's message for you, it should start to affect your heart, soul, and mind. The promise of heaven should get your heart beating a little faster. It should cause you to take an inventory of the way you're using your time, treasure, and talents. Ask yourself regularly, "Where do my passions lie and what truly motivates me?" The more you and I expose ourselves to this undeniable truth, the more we'll want to live for Christ. This is when I realize just how much I love Him and want to serve Him and put away that which hinders and entangles (Hebrews 12:2) and spend myself for Him and Him alone.

If only the Church would heed this call, if we would put down our little idols and useless pursuits and embrace with true passion the beauty and glory and majesty that is only found in Jesus Christ. Just imagine with me if one by one we decided to act on this truth and just took God at His Word! Imagine living as if God means what He says. Think about the way prayers would change, how songs would be sung, what love would be felt, how mission and church-planting would explode, how the gospel would go forth, and what resources would pour from heaven to God's people. If only the Church took up its calling for true passion which the Lord has so clearly put before us in His Word.

Oh Lord, forgive us for being so idolatrous and blind, and frankly for being so stupid. Forgive us, Lord. Yet there's still time. Do you sense that? There's still time for you and for me. Our passion can truly be heaven and our love can fully be Christ. No wonder I love to sing songs and hymns with final verses like this:

Oh Lord, haste the day when my faith shall be sight,
The clouds be rolled back as a scroll;

The trump shall resound, and the Lord shall descend,
Even so it is well with my soul.[22]

You better believe it's well with my soul. There's nothing better. That day is coming soon and oh so soon. Are you ready? Is your heavenly passport close by?

When the nearness of heaven is realized, power and fruitfulness are also close at hand. That anticipation is why it's good to groan, because we were made for something more.

C.S. Lewis brilliantly described the vision of eternity through the voice of Jewel, the horse, in his book *The Last Battle*:

I have come home at last! This is my real country! I belong here. This is the land I have been looking for all my life, though I never knew it till now... Come further up, come further in![23]

**FURTHER THOUGHT AND REFLECTION:**
**PREPARING FOR ETERNITY**
You may ask, "What do I do to live with eternity in mind? I want to grow in this very much." Good! Me too. Let's consider the following:

- Memorize a passage of Scripture that renews your mind in this exact truth (Philippians 3; Romans 8; Hebrews 13). Once memorized, it has the potential to carry you right through to eternity. That's awesome!
- Write down somewhere obvious the phrase "Astra Petamus," and pray that you would be a man or woman who seeks heaven.
- Convince yourself that this world is not all there is. As wonderful as some of it is, the world and our time in it is

temporary. Use that truth to motivate you towards what is: eternity!

- When your body groans, let it remind you of the glorious truth that you were not ultimately made for this world.
- Find a song whose lyrics speak of eternity right now. Play it loud and sing it loud.

## CHAPTER SIX
The Purity of Passion: Success

*Seek first the kingdom of God and his righteousness, and all these things will be added to you.*

—Matthew 6:33

The worst thing that can happen to a man is for him to succeed before he is ready.[24]

—Martyn Lloyd-Jones

The world links passion and success closely together—find your passion and success will follow. But so many pastors, leaders, and believers are led astray by their definition of success without taking the time to hear the Lord's opinion on the matter. The temptation is to hold up our own definition of success, dress it up with Christianese, and convince ourselves we are on the right track. All the while we quite possibly drift further away from the will of God and quench the power of God's Spirit in our lives. And when we quench God's Spirit, we lose our passion and zeal for God.

Let's be honest: too many pastors and church leaders have swallowed hook, line, and sinker a definition of success that is flat-out unbiblical. However, I understand how they/we/I can be led off course. Day in and day out, we are fed unrelenting messages of worldly success. By far, most leaders believe success is found in attendance numbers, expanding financials, larger buildings, and speaking platforms. They measure their success based on Twitter followers, podcast downloads, and overall popularity. We convince ourselves that God's success is found exclusively in these numbers. Worse, we find that our happiness rises and falls based on how we perceive ourselves and how other people perceive us. We chase greater statistics that boost our self-esteem and promote our own importance. That is exhausting, crushing, and downright sinful.

But here's a question: what if our definition of success was actually unbiblical? What if, despite our good intentions, we find ourselves climbing the wrong ladder of success? Wouldn't it be helpful and freeing to discover and live by a definition of success that God has guaranteed to bless?

Well, listen closely. It *is* possible, and it's exactly what the Lord wants for you and me. He doesn't want us chasing and consuming self-promotion and self-glory disguised as leadership principles to grow a church. No. He wants us to know His heart for leaders within the church. This is precisely where true success is found.

Admittedly, we are entering territory which could fill another whole book, but let's keep to the basics and identify true biblical success. My "success" items are not exhaustive, but I believe they are supported by Scripture and produce tremendous freedom and fruitfulness in our lives, because true success is that which God blesses, no matter how the world measures the results.

Over the years, the question I keep asking myself is this: what are the things that God blesses? The answer defines true,

Christ-centred success. Such a simple question, yet it has such life-changing consequences.

Below is a list I have called "When in doubt, do this." In other words, when all else fails, when anxiety takes over, when stress keeps me awake at night, when opposition arises, when the attack of the enemy is brutal, when I feel most discouraged and lost, or when I'm most tempted towards pride, what will be my response? What is my go-to plan? What do I believe most pleases God?

Here's the truth and the secret to this definition of success: when I'm doing that which I know God guarantees to bless, I know I'm good. As in, I know I'm in His will and I know I'm where He wants me to be. Pursuing success this way takes all the guesswork out of the equation. I don't have to wonder, worry, or fret. I am pursuing that which He says He will dwell within, and therefore peace fills my soul—and success fills my life.

God guarantees to bless the following:

- God blesses love for Him: adoration (Deuteronomy 6:5; Matthew 22:37).
- God blesses true brokenness and repentance: humility (Isaiah 57:15; Psalm 51:17).
- God blesses dependence upon Him: prayer (John 15:7; Hebrews 4:16).
- God blesses the exaltation of Him: glory (Isaiah 42:8; John 4:24).
- God blesses humility before Him: worship (Isaiah 66:2; James 4:2).
- God blesses holiness in Him: obedience (2 Corinthians 7:1; Ephesians 4:24; 1 Thessalonians 4:4).
- God blesses a hunger for Him: reliance (Psalm 42:1; Matthew 5:6).

The point I'm trying to make is that when all else fails and this becomes my to-do list, I'm guaranteed to be in hot pursuit of the will of God, because God tells me so clearly in His Word what He blesses. If I start with this heart for Him, I can't go wrong. When I wake up and my actions are love for God, dependence in prayer, intentional pursuit of humility, longing for holiness, and meditation of His Word, I am successful in the eyes of God.

But you might say, "Well, that is so simple and basic." I would wholeheartedly agree. We are the ones who complicate things with our self-motivated desires for unbiblical success. We talk about love for God, the need for prayer, and pursuit of holiness, but do those values really define our lives? Or it is lip service while we pursue our true goals of self-glory? I want you to stop right now and honestly ask yourself the following questions. What is your definition of success? What are your goals and ambitions? It's just you and God right now, so why not admit where and how your idea of success doesn't line up with God's?

I've watched many powerful and well-known Christian leaders fall from their high pedestals. There is much attention, focus, admiration, and hype on these splashy individuals who, when it is all said and done, might not even finish well, if at all. You tell me: is that success? As John Piper powerfully stated, "The world does not need another entrepreneurial pastor but a more humbly holy, heart-penetrating portrayer of the Son of God."[25] We have enough of the entrepreneurs. Now we need to see some holiness in our leaders.

As I watch across the landscape of Christian leadership, more than ever I look hard for those men and women who stand the test of time and finish well. Let me say that again: those who finish well. I have the utmost respect and admiration for the man who served the Lord with all his heart for decade after decade and joined with Paul in saying, *"I have fought the good fight, I have finished the race, I have kept the faith"* (2 Timothy 4:7). In most cases, these are not the most gifted or well-known individuals, but to me they are powerfully successful. They are not perfect, but they loved their God, were faithful to their spouses, were examples to their children, and were pastors to their churches. They had deficiencies like us all, but they withstood the test of time, persevered, and were powerfully used of God in their own way. To me, that is wonderful success.

Consider this powerful quote on the life of D.L. Moody:

How many men whom God has led out and greatly used in America have become puffed up, and God has to lay them aside; but Mr. Moody was never laid aside. God used him to the end.[26]

The words "and God has to lay them aside" hit me hard. This is something rarely discussed in our Christian celebrity culture, but it needs to be.

I've long been captured by Revelation 2:5, where Jesus says so clearly to the Church in Ephesus,

*Remember therefore from where you have fallen; repent, and do the works you did at first. If not, I will come to you and remove your lampstand from its place, unless you repent.*

Consider how seriously God takes His Church and the purity of leadership within it. How many individuals, churches, and denominations have had their "lampstand" removed and been left stunned and humiliated? How many have settled for their own version of success? Please, Lord, not us.

At this point, critics might argue that those who stand against the common understanding of success do so because they lack success. These critics often argue that leaders with little success form theologies to support their little growth, or altogether lack of growth. That may be true in some cases, but I am resolved as ever to pursue true success, and I am part of a ministry that would be deemed quite successful by modern standards. The church I pastor began with two couples, and my wife and I were one of them. Just over a decade later, our church has several thousand in attendance, has planted several thriving churches, and has a growing influence across our region and nation.

But please hear me, because it's hard for me to even write the previous sentence for fear that it may be perceived as pride. My point is that despite great success, more than ever I want to experience true success in the eyes of God. I live to see lives being changed for the glory of God. I am more committed than ever to pursuing Him above all, because that's where I am most free! When I am filled with genuine worship of my Saviour and on my knees in prayer, believing in the power of humility, I know I'm where I need to be. I don't have to worry about human measurements or paralyzing insecurities, because I'm too preoccupied with fixing my eyes on Jesus. And believe me, this does result in wonderful, life-changing freedom. I encourage you to thoughtfully define, declare, and devote yourself to God's definition of success for a week or two and see how it goes. I guarantee you'll be blessed, because you'll be with God.

I began this chapter with a quote from Martyn Lloyd-Jones—"The worst thing that can happen to a man is for him to find success before he is ready."[27] The success that Lloyd-Jones is referring to is what most Christian leaders long for and lust after. We want influence, fruitfulness, and impact. But Lloyd-Jones' wisdom here is profound. So often the very thing we want most is what we are unable to handle. If given what we really want, it would ruin us.

## NINETY YEARS OF WISDOM

The following is an excerpt from the autobiography of a man named Harold Burchett. I have never met Pastor Burchett, but he has been a mentor to one of my mentors. A section in the preface of his book made me sit in silence for several minutes. For context, Pastor Burchett is currently in his nineties and is "looking back over more than eighty years of seeing God work."[28] That's right, over eighty years! Wow. Read and absorb his precious advice:

> Through it all, I can see now that God has employed several protective barriers to guard me from possible spiritual failure and disaster:
> 1. All through my maturing years I was kept from gaining money. Here was a responsibility I did not have!
> 2. I was kept from public notice—a burden I did not bear.
> 3. In my older years I was given an ongoing lock-in with my wife's Alzheimer's Disease. This weakening seclusion promoted spiritual insight and strength. I did not attain it all, but I was more hedged in and directed towards God's goal.[29]

When I finished reading this, I had to sit, be still, and think for a long time. The reason for my extended pause was that I knew the reality of what most pastors and leaders actually want from this life. It seriously made me pause over my own heart and life.

Our Western culture and overemphasis on achievement-driven leadership has convinced pastors that success comes in specific forms. I believe that if pastors and leaders were totally honest as they look ahead, the very things they would aspire towards in some form or another would be the things Pastor Burchett said God protected him from! That's not insignificant to me. Pastors and leaders would probably never say it out loud, because we're too smart to be that honest. However, the ambition in the Western Church is often rooted in financial gain, public notoriety, and an overall freedom from serious pain and trial. Please read that again. Can you and I admit that so much of the culture we are immersed in, even sadly within the Church, revolves around standards of measurement that might be opposed to the very will of God?

The grace of God upon Harold Burchett's life as he looked back over eighty years of ministry is that God spared him from too much money, too much fame, and God *did* give him significant pain and trial. This, in his opinion, is how God allowed him to be successful. Trust me, if you can make it through eight decades of ministry without major failures or disaster, *that* would be success!

## GOD'S GREAT PARADOX

This then is God's great paradox: how does He bless a man without ruining him? The answer is rooted in getting your definition of success in line with God's. When this truly happens, you cannot lose. And the reason you cannot lose is because you are constantly seeking to decrease that Christ might increase (John 3:30). Once again, that is true success!

Are you and I able right now to choose a path of true humility by repenting of a worldly view of success? Are you and I able right now to admit our sin before God that we have believed lies that have actually weakened God's power through our lives? Are you and I able to own the fact that we have used politically and spiritually correct language but in reality sought the path of our own glory?

I know this level of honesty may hurt, but are you wise enough to understand that this is the beginning of true success? Can you see how this is the very path to getting back on God's plan and receiving God's blessing? Is the Lord giving you eyes to recognize once again that His will and His fruit are different than the world's? Even within some portions of the Church?

Again, we must get to the point we have already defined and become convinced deep in our hearts about what God truly blesses so that when we are most conflicted, fearful, and confused, we will be able to tell ourselves, "When in doubt, do this!" It's not a formula, but a biblical pattern of wisdom that leads us to the throne of grace… guaranteed!

## FURTHER THOUGHT AND REFLECTION: A PRAYER FOR TRUE SUCCESS

Oh Lord, may our passion for success be defined by and guided by You. Forgive us, Lord, for all our selfish ambition, self-promotion, and self-glory. Have mercy on us for how we use Your name to draw attention to ourselves and to overcome our own insecurities. Oh God, may You lead us to higher ground. May You renew our minds to be cleansed of worldly measurements of success and instead fill us with a tremendous passion for Christ-centred, humility-producing, God-glorifying success. Yes, Lord, allow us to taste how satisfying and peace-producing Your ways truly are. Raise up a generation of men and women who love You far more than themselves. May it be so in Jesus' name. Amen!

Those who do away with Christian doctrine are, whether they are aware of it or not, the worst enemies of Christian living ... [because] the coals of orthodoxy are necessary to the fire of piety.[30]

—Charles Spurgeon

*Your words were found, and I ate them, and your words became to me a joy and the delight of my heart, for I am called by your name, O Lord, God of hosts.*

—Jeremiah 15:16

It has been said that Charles Spurgeon once spoke the following: "A Bible that's falling apart usually belongs to someone who isn't." I have always loved that quote. It speaks of the inescapable truth that genuine Christian maturity cannot occur apart from the Word of God.

We also know that genuine Christian passion cannot occur apart from the Word of God. This is why Jesus prayed to His Father for the Church in John 17:17: *"Sanctify them in the truth; your word is truth."* Jesus prayed this because He knew perfectly well that without His Word we will not grow. The Word of God is God's special revelation to His Church. The Word of God alone tells us who God is and what He's done in redemptive history. The Word of God alone steers us from error, grows us in sanctification, renews our minds, and points us to a life of fruitfulness and purpose. John MacArthur once said at a conference that some books change a person's thinking, but only one book can change that person's nature. Exactly.

## YOU CAN'T TRULY LOVE GOD
## UNLESS YOU TRULY KNOW GOD

The fundamental reason that truth is essential is that it's the pathway to knowing God. Can you truly love someone without knowing them? Can I fully love my wife without a comprehensive understanding of her character, personality, and likes and dislikes? True love in relationship comes through true knowledge of a person. The same is true with God. If we don't truly know Him, how can we truly love Him? That is why He has given us His Word, His truth. Because to truly know Him is to truly love Him.

Why did the Psalmist declare, *"With my whole heart I seek you; let me not wander from your commandments!"* (Psalm 119:10)? Because seeking the Lord is inseparable from seeking His truth. This is why the Psalmist also proclaimed, *"I have stored up your word in my heart, that I might not sin against you"* (Psalm 119:11). Think about what this verse is saying. It's the Word of God within us that renews our thinking and directs us by God's Spirit. We begin to see sin diminished in our lives when God's Word is active in our minds. And when God's Word is active in our lives, our love for God increases. Conversely, when sin grows in our lives, God's Spirit is grieved, our love for the Lord decreases, and our passion and zeal goes with it. Furthermore, when we go to the New Testament, we read one of the most powerful verses in Scripture:

*All Scripture is breathed out by God and profitable for teaching, for reproof, for correction, and for training in righteousness, that the man of God may be complete, equipped for every good work.* (2 Timothy 3:16–17)

Think about that! Please, look at that truth. The Word of God is undeniably essential for all forms of maturity in Christ. I know I've already said that, but hear it again. Too many believers lack passion because they lack or ignore truth.

## WHAT IS THEOLOGY ANYWAY?

Just consider the word "theology." It comes from two Greek words: *theos*, meaning God, and *logos*, meaning word. Therefore, the study of theology is ultimately the study of God. In its purest form, it is a tremendous hunger to know God more. Yes, theology can be abused, misapplied, and turned towards legalism or empty intellectual exercises. However, with a pure heart and humble mind, theology sets a person on fire for the Lord Jesus Christ.

When a person truly grasps the truth of God, they cannot stop their zeal for God. I constantly remind our people and those whom I disciple that the purpose of theology is not just information, but transformation. I have a strong distaste for intellectual Bible-heads who lack passion for Christ. It becomes all thought and no heart. This cannot be! I love how Paul Tripp puts it. He explains that these individuals have "big theological brains" yet are left with "heart disease."[31]

A large Bible-brain with no heart does not produce true theology. True theology means acquiring knowledge of God in order to acquire passion for God and practice obedience to Him. This is why some of my favourite worship songs are deep theological songs. They combine the awesome and deep truth of Scripture with a passionate expression of love. Here's one I'm particularly thankful for right now. It's old, but many new songs equally speak truth and are used by God to renew our minds.

> There is a fountain filled with blood
> drawn from Emmanuel's veins;
> And sinners plunged beneath that flood
> lose all their guilty stains.
> E'er since, by faith, I saw the stream
> Thy flowing wounds supply,
> Redeeming love has been my theme,
> and shall be till I die.[32]

How powerful it is to have the depth of theology sung with passion of the soul. This is what truth is supposed to do. It's supposed to throw logs on our fire for Christ. This is the true theologian: someone pursuing the glory of God with their head and their heart.

### ARE YOU A THEOLOGIAN?

As you read that subtitle, I hope you're answering, "Yes, I am." A theologian is not some balding old guy wearing a bowtie and sitting in a cave of an office with books stacked to the ceiling. I believe that every true follower of Christ is called to be a theologian of sorts.

Now, I understand that there are certain men and women who are called and set apart for special study of doctrine on a scholarly level. However, I believe that as the Church we have left the pursuit of God to too few. We have claimed that pursuing God in this way is up to others, giving us an excuse for compromise. This attitude needs to change. Theology is part of authentic discipleship—you're not following Jesus if your theology isn't improving in breadth and depth. This concern is a huge part of the motivation behind this book, to convince you toward a passion for God's Word that results in a passion for God Himself. This is the ultimate pursuit of the true theologian.

So all of us should have the title "theologian" on our resume. This is not boasting; this is our calling. I call and empower you to the task of being a theologian. I pray this very week that you will begin to wake up early with an extra special focus and desire to pursue the Lord in truth. Maybe as you rise, one of your children or your spouse will ask, "What are you doing?" And you will answer, "I'm practicing being a theologian." Amen, brother or sister. Go hard after God and His truth, believing He will not let you down, ever.

## THE POWER OF PASSION FOR THE TRUTH

A passage that is paramount in understanding and unpacking a passion for truth is Hebrews 5:11–6:1.

> *About this we have much to say, and it is hard to explain, since you have become dull of hearing. For though by this time you ought to be teachers, you need someone to teach you again the basic principles of the oracles of God. You need milk, not solid food, for everyone who lives on milk is unskilled in the word of righteousness, since he is a child. But solid food is for the mature, for those who have their powers of discernment trained by constant practice to distinguish good from evil.*

> *Therefore let us leave the elementary doctrine of Christ and go on to maturity, not laying again a foundation of repentance from dead works and of faith toward God…*

I just love this text because it pinpoints the need for truth, the blessing of truth, and then warns us of the danger in lacking truth. I want you to carefully notice three things about this passage:

**1. You have the problem.** The author of Hebrews explains that the believers are not growing. He says that they have become *"dull of hearing"* when they should be teachers.

Understand that to be *"dull of hearing"* is not an ear problem but rather a heart problem. A lack of hunger for the Lord and His Word is fundamentally a heart problem.

The people the author is talking about should have been teachers of the Word by then, but instead they were still on Pablum; they needed to be weaned off. But notice the devastation of not growing in the Word of God. The text says that the people were *"unskilled in the word of righteousness."* This means that they were not able to handle the sword of the Spirit effectively. They should have been sword masters, but instead they were quite unskilled.

The author is indicating that the believers had remained children and therefore were vulnerable to attack. Consider a young child's vulnerability. Young children will believe anything you tell them. Trust me, I have four children and I've tried this. Young children don't know any better. It's not their fault they are so naïve, ignorant, and helpless; it's our task as parents not to leave them in that state.

Consider the youngest of babies. They will put anything in their mouths with no comprehension of whether the item will even cause their own death. Why? Because they simply do not know. They are ignorant of the truth or lie in front of them.

The devastation the writer was confronting is widespread throughout the Christian Church today. There are so many immature, ignorant believers who simply don't know what is right from wrong, and therefore they find themselves in great danger. A passion for truth is a massive step in defence against ignorance, and more importantly against evil. You have a problem if you are theologically immature.

**2. You have the prescription.** The author doesn't waste words. He says that it's time for the Church to grow up. But how are they to grow? By eating, of course. But eating what? By feeding on the Word of God. The *"solid food"* prescribed here is the truth and doctrines of God's Word. The life that is built by feeding on God's truth and living out God's truth is following God's prescription for godly living.

**3. You have the plea.** The plea of the author is to grow up! Why? Because life is too short not to grow in Jesus Christ. It saddens me to think how many believers will stand before the Lord and be asked to give an account of what they've done with what God has entrusted to them. How many will be without excuse, because God has given them everything they needed?

I am convinced that many believers will stand before the Lord and realize for the first time just how powerful God's Word could have been in their lives and how much they've missed, simply because they didn't read it. If you know God's Word, you will also know just how many passages, parables, and exhortations revolve around not wasting your opportunity. Jesus went out of His way to warn us over and over again to make the most of what we've been given. He pleads with His disciples to not waste our lives. The author of Hebrews does the same.

Hebrews 5:14 emphasizes the importance of growth: *"But solid food is for the mature, for those who have their powers of discernment trained by constant practice to distinguish good from evil."* This is why so many believers have never graduated from elementary school. They simply don't know the Word; they don't know doctrine, and therefore they don't fully know the Lord.

What burdens me deeply is that in many cases the Church is not teaching them or feeding them with solid food. I have heard countless testimonies from people who couldn't take any more of "not being fed." They are famished for truth, desperate for growth in Christ, and the Holy Spirit within them is giving them a hunger for solid spiritual food. Of course He is, because we can't truly love God unless we truly know God.

Notice from this passage that the Word of God brings maturity, discernment, wisdom, sustenance, strength, and stability. But if this is the result of feeding on God's truth, what happens if you remove or ignore it? A church without passion for the truth wanders, and believers without passion for the truth are immature, foolish, weak, malnourished, unwise, naïve, and unstable followers of Jesus. That description leads to one of the greatest dangers threatening the Church today, and one of the greatest killers of passion in the Church.

I trust you're seeing the effects of passion for truth. It's so beautiful and powerful, and God uses it to grow us in every way! It's shocking in our day that such large sections of the Church are seemingly afraid of truth. They apologize for God's truth, avoid God's truth, minimize God's truth, and water down God's truth. But let's be clear: if you're afraid of God's truth, you're afraid of maturity in Christ.

## ABUSED BY TRUTH

With the above challenge ringing in our ears, here's what I know to be the experience for some of you reading this right now: in your past, you've been abused by truth. You grew up in a hard, cold, legalistic environment where truth was used as a weapon of guilt and autocracy. Some of you were under the leadership of those who supposedly loved the truth but were harsh, lacked grace, and were devoid of love. I understand this and I have seen this. I'm truly sorry for your pain, but I beg you to hear me. Let us never allow the abuses of a few become an obstacle against what's true. I have seen too many believers overreact to abuse of truth by swinging all the way over to a distortion of grace, to the point of an altogether absence of truth. This is not right, either. Jesus was, after all, our perfect example of grace *and* truth (John 1:14). Jesus, without a doubt, loved truth. Let us be the same, pursuing grace and truth.

As Eric Thoenes says, "Knowledge without devotion is cold, dead orthodoxy, but devotion without knowledge is irrational instability."[33] So good and so true. The point of this whole chapter, and the underlying goal of this book, is to encourage you toward a knowledge of God accompanied by great devotion. Yes, Lord, may it be so!

## THE POWER OF THE RENEWING OF YOUR MIND

Why is passion for the truth so vital? Beyond the reasons I have already provided, it's the truth that renews our mind. It's difficult to overstate the importance of mind renewal in the Christian life. Consider Romans 12:2:

> *Do not be conformed to this world, but be transformed by* the renewal of your mind*, that by testing you may discern what is the will of God, what is good and acceptable and perfect.* (emphasis added)

Notice that true transformation comes by the renewal of the mind. Notice also that through renewing our minds with God's Word, we are able to discern the will of God. So again, imagine with me what happens if a believer chooses not to renew their mind on a daily basis. They are essentially choosing not to be transformed, not to know God's will, to not be aware of what's *"good acceptable and perfect."* What true believer would actually choose not to grow? But every time we fail to pursue a passion for truth, we fail to pursue all these truths.

Mind renewal has always been one of my top five convictions, simply because the mind is a crucial part of our relationship with God. Jesus made loving God with our mind part of the Great Commandment (Mark 12:30). Let's reinforce this brilliant and beautiful truth.

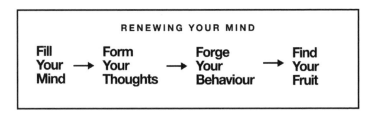

Review that chart and see the flow of power in mind renewal. What we fill our minds with determines what we think about, what we think about leads to our behaviour, and how we behave ultimately determines the fruit from our lives. Again, this is why Jesus prayed to His Father, *"Sanctify them in the truth; your word is truth"* (John 17:17). We don't stand a chance apart from the renewal of our minds.

Isn't this exciting, though? Isn't this a fresh and challenging way to look at the importance of God's truth in our lives? Let these thoughts lead you to a great prayer for a passion for truth and mind renewal.

## A POEM OF MIND RENEWAL

I want to share something very dear to me. The following is a poem from my great-grandmother, Winifred Symons. This poem has been on display in my parents' house for many years and has always been a source of great blessing and encouragement, and you're about to realize why. It was first written by hand in my great-grandmother's prayer book:

O Lord renew in me today
A mind to please thee well
That seeks not high things but doth choose
In lowliness to dwell.
Thy mind O Christ, Which for my sin
Led thee to Calvary
Impart to me today I pray
That I may live for thee.
Help me to think on all things pure
Things honest, lovely, true
Since in myself O Lord I fall
Thy mind in me renew.

Can I get an amen for Granny Symons? I find that to be beautiful and ever so meaningful. I hope you do, too.

## THE BIBLE IS NOT AN ITEM ON YOUR CHECKLIST

So, after all this truth on the passion of truth, without a doubt you are thinking, *I'm convinced, but what do I do?* This final section is to set you on a path of powerful mind renewal, deepening your passion for the truth.

First, you must start by knowing and living this: the Bible is not an item on your checklist, but rather the Bible is life! Way too many believers approach God's Word as a chore to be done at some point in the day. They sit down with a grumpy and lazy attitude and simply want to go through their readings to appease their guilt and then get on with their day. How often do you and I begin to read God's Word while already looking forward to picking up our smartphone, tablet, or computer to get to the *real* important stuff of the day?

Stop for a second and think about this. As we've been learning, distracted discipleship is not an ear or eye problem; it's a *heart* problem. Any person who sees their time in the Word of God as a checklist item needs to get a new theology, because they're totally missing out on what's actually true. They need to understand that the Bible is our source of transformation in Jesus Christ. Don't wake up and anticipate a chore in God's Word. No, let's pray that we wake up and anticipate an encounter with the living God! Now *that* sounds life-giving and exciting! And living, energizing food for our souls is exactly what God's Word is supposed to be.

## THE WORD ON THE WORD

I've always found that my passion for God's Word and for God Himself grows as I read, study, and meditate on Psalm 19:7–8:

> *The law of the Lord is perfect,* reviving *the soul; the testimony of the Lord is sure,* making wise *the simple; the precepts of the Lord are right,* rejoicing *the heart; the commandment of the Lord is pure,* enlightening *the eyes. (emphasis added)*

The perfect law of God *revives* the soul. It's what God uses to quicken the unbeliever to life and call back the complacent to passion. This is why the preaching and study of God's Word are massively important. It revives our souls. Yes, Lord!

But then we also read that it makes the simple *wise*. How beautiful that all true life-giving wisdom is found in the Word of God. Don't ever underestimate the precious nature of God's wisdom found in the pages of your Bible. To know the path of eternal life and godliness is to know the wisdom of God's Word.

Then the psalm says that the precepts of the Lord cause the heart to *rejoice*. Thank You, Lord, that this is true. This happened to me this morning... again! I opened God's Word and sought to open my heart. As the truth permeated my soul, it surely caused my heart to rejoice. This is because the Bible is a supernatural book that God uses to renew our minds and lead our hearts to Him. And when you're led to Him, there is only joy to be found. How awesome is God's truth!

Finally, *"the commandment of the Lord is pure, <u>enlightening the eyes."</u>* The Word causes us to truly see in the midst of such a dark world. When fear, anxiety, stress, and despair tempt us, the truth of God sets our minds straight.

Right now, as I look across the landscape of the globe and all the hate, fragility, uncertainty, and chaos, verses like Isaiah 33:6 allow me to truly see: *"and he will be the stability of your times."* No matter how awful this world seemingly becomes, God is our refuge, our strength, and the stability of our times. And that's just one small phrase among thousands designed by God to enlighten our eyes so we can truly see. Oh God, give us a passion for truth.

But again, I can hear some saying, "Okay, I get it, but help me. Where do I start? How do I start in growing passion for God's truth?" Let's get very practical.

**1. Get a plan.** You must have a plan to read God's Word. Winston Churchill once said, "Failing to plan is planning to fail." Without a plan for engaging with God's Word, we are subject to distraction and wandering. I hear this all the time from believers. Decide today to get a plan that you can keep, and stick with it. This isn't to be legalistic, but rather to be realistic. Plans work.[34]

**2. Get a place.** I just love "my place." My place consists of a special chair with a well-worn ottoman in a special corner of our house. I visit it virtually every morning quite early, before the rascals wake up. It's my place to meet with God, to pursue Him, to love Him, and to hear from Him to allow my mind to be renewed as each day begins. This place is my lifeline in Jesus Christ. I admit that I love routine, but hear the heart behind this: the place is not a temple, but rather where I take my temple to prepare it to be put to *"honorable use"* (2 Timothy 2:21). I highly recommend finding your place.

**3. Get a pen (and paper).** Once you have your plan and your place, it's time to get a pen. Why? So you can write down observations, passions, and prayers. I have been journaling in some form or another ever since I got saved. I don't journal every single day, but I do it often and it's a way of putting on paper what the Lord speaks to my heart. Journaling becomes a spiritual discipline in my passion for truth and for the Lord. I've had several journals over the years, and they have proven to be great sources of encouragement to me, especially when dark times come. In your passion for truth, get a pen.

**4. Get a prayer.** This is most important and will lead us into the next chapter. I love when the psalmist prays, *"Open my eyes, that I may behold wondrous things out of your law"* (Psalm 119:18). He is asking for revelation and insight. It's a prayer that your time with the Lord will truly be supernatural. It's a request that could change your life on a daily basis. On that note, develop a prayer for hunger for the Lord, for passion of His Word, for resolve throughout your life. When I am closest in intimacy to the Lord, I find that I can't wait to get to bed early so I can wake up early. I'm such a morning person that when

I'm filled with such love for Christ, I eagerly await daybreak to come so I can seek Him again. Oh what a joy to be in this place. This can happen to you, too.

**5. Get a passion.** These steps are not a formula built in religion; they are a proven way that thousands of believers have walked before you in intimacy with God. When these steps are combined with a sincere and humble heart, passion is just around the corner. When you sow the seeds of a longing for God's truth, you will soon reap the harvest of true passion. This has always been and this will always be. You will anticipate joining with the psalmist, who says, *"I will never forget your precepts, for by them you have given me life"* (Psalm 119:93). Amen.

## CHAPTER EIGHT
The Power of Passion: Prayer

*If you abide in me, and my words abide in you, ask whatever you wish, and it will be done for you.*

—John 15:7

Nothing distinguishes the children of God so clearly and strongly as prayer. It is the one infallible mark and test of being a Christian.[35]

—E.M. Bounds

A phrase you'll hear often around our church family is "Without prayer, we're dead." Why? Because it's true! Prayer in its most basic form and definition is an earnest plea. It's a cry for help, an admission that you cannot do it on your own and eagerly desire assistance. Therefore, a profoundly simple yet theologically clear prayer is: *I need you, God!*

Conversely, though, a prayerless life, whether we mean to communicate this attitude or not, is a life that says, *I don't need you, God.* Think about that truth for a moment. A failure to pray as an individual, family, or church is in some way saying, *Thanks, God, but we got this one.* I would be hard-pressed to find a believer who would admit to that statement, but that's exactly what we communicate to the Lord when we fail to pray.

Our actions prove that we do not believe in the power of prayer, or maybe more accurately, we believe more in the power of self. This is an area where we must increasingly allow our theology to truly become our practice. We must convince ourselves through the renewal of our minds that if we fail to pray, we fail to invite God's power to be seen in and through our lives.

If this last statement doesn't resonate, you may need to reread the last chapter.

## APART FROM ME YOU CAN DO NOTHING

John 15:5 contains a statement of truth constructed from seven life-changing and mind-blowing words. Jesus said that *"apart from [him] you can do nothing."* Last time I checked, nothing meant… well, nothing!

Two verses later, Jesus declares, *"If you abide in me, and my words abide in you, ask whatever you wish, and it will be done for you"* (John 15:7). Notice the crystal clear connection between *abiding* and *prayer*. Abiding in the One who can do all things leads us to powerful, passionate prayer. This principle is so simple, yet so profound.

I have seen many church gatherings, congregational business meetings, and church leadership meetings begin with what I can only describe as a perfunctory prayer before they quickly move on to the agenda. Theologically, this is crazy. They don't have their theology right, because if they did, they would insist on earnest and passionate prayer. Prayer isn't scheduled first to get it out of the way; it's first because little may need to be said after the prayer, once we realize with whom we are talking and what He may be trying to tell us. There are no exceptions to this spiritual rule—apart from God, you can do nothing.

## WE DON'T KNOW WHAT WE ARE DOING

This phrase is the Old Testament equivalent of John 15:5. It's taken from the powerful story of Jehoshaphat found in 2 Chronicles 20 and has become the theme of the elders board within our church.

In the early years of our church, when we were less than one year old, we elders found ourselves often admitting to one another, "We don't know what we're doing." We said that partially in jest, yet with deadly seriousness about the limits of our wisdom versus God's wisdom. One of my elders would go on to say, "We didn't get this far by being smart." In other words, our ingenuity hasn't resulted in the fruit we've seen. No, it's been the grace, wisdom, and power of God.

During my summer break in the first year of our church, I found myself reading through 2 Chronicles and learning more about the trials and triumphs (mostly trials) of the Kingdom of Judah. I was reflecting on our church when I reached the story of Jehoshaphat. I read it with fresh eyes and tremendous excitement. I felt a tectonic shift in my thinking as I read the following passage:

> O our God, will you not execute judgment on them? For we are powerless against this great horde that is coming against us. We do not know what to do, but our eyes are on you. (2 Chronicles 20:12 emphasis added).

The last sentence struck me as if for the first time. I quickly grabbed my journal and wrote down that I had found the theme verse for our elders! Later, my leaders and I shared in the joy of seeing how biblical it is to keep our eyes fixed upon the Lord in total dependence when we don't know what we're doing.

This statement by Jehoshaphat is part of a king's public prayer. It's the final petition to the Lord within a desperate cry for help and deliverance. Jehoshaphat sees his enemies approaching; a great horde is coming against them. He knows he is helpless, weak, and unable to defeat those enemies without the power, wisdom, and glory of his God. Therefore, with complete humility, dependence, desperation, and passion, he calls out, *"We do not know what to do, but our eyes are on you."* If you don't love that admission yet, watch what happens next. The account says that *"all Judah stood before the Lord, with their little ones, their wives, and their children. And the Spirit of the Lord came upon [them]..."* (2 Chronicles 20:13–14) Exactly. God's Spirit caused one (Jahaziel) to speak, and all (including the king) to listen, worship, and respond.

Just as on that day in Jerusalem, an all-out commitment and dependence on the Lord in prayer still ushers in His grace, power, and ultimate deliverance. Follow this passage to the end and you will see an incredible demonstration of God's power and deliverance. Notice the resolute call for strength among God's people and for their faith (2 Chronicles 20:15–17). See an entire community of God's people fall down in authentic, humble worship (2 Chronicles 20:18–19). Feel the growing momentum of faith among the leadership, leading to supernatural boldness and courage in the face of tremendous opposition (2 Chronicles 20:20). Notice the crystal clear focus on the character and promises of God, and then imagine the scene as the people begin to march, singing to their awesome God. Then the Lord does what only the Lord can do. This verse is so fantastic, I must quote it in full:

*And when they began to sing and praise, the Lord set an ambush against the men of Ammon, Moab, and Mount Seir, who had come against Judah, so that they were routed.* (2 Chronicles 20:22)

How awesome is that? As they began to sing and praise the Lord, He brought an incredible victory that is recorded for all time. And let's remember that all of this started with a passionate, humility-filled prayer of *"We do not know what to do, but our eyes are on you."* That's it. That dependence on God provides the true leadership so desperately needed in our day. It's a passion for prayer, solely and completely rooted in the power and grace of the Lord. After all, apart from Christ we can do nothing.

Please understand, I'm not arguing for having no knowledge or avoiding decisions, but I am arguing for the starting point of desperation, brokenness, and humility. That attitude defines the heart, the leader, and the Church that God will bless without question.

I can't tell you how moved and encouraged our church body is to hear "We don't know what we're doing" coming from their elders. You can almost hear the sigh of relief that another leader isn't going to stand before them and give them the impression that they've got it all figured out. I'm repelled by leaders who do that, simply because they're lying! Anyone who portrays a smug "I've got it all together" type of attitude is a fraud and everyone seems to know it but them. The congregations of today long for leaders who will relate to them by admitting that they don't have all the answers, but they're fixing their eyes on the One who does.

I find this truth to be most freeing, peace-giving, and helpful in times of anxiety and stress. How often do I come to a place where my wisdom, strength, and ideas are not enough? All the time! It is precisely when I'm faced with all the pressure of leading that I must fall on my knees in prayer and cry out, "God, I don't know what to do, but my eyes are on You."

Over and over again this has proved to be my turning point as a leader. Over and over this has ushered in the grace of God, the presence of God, the wisdom of God, the strength of God, and the glory of God upon my life and ministry. God promises to give grace to the humble, and the starting point for the humble is "I don't have a clue" and "Apart from Christ I know I can do nothing."

The leaders within our church have become so convinced of this foundation of prayer and leadership that we have placed this verse in our board room and even had T-shirts made that say "We don't know what we're doing" on the front, with the text of 2 Chronicles 20:12 on the back. This starting point results in serious spiritual momentum, because God works in the people, the leadership, and the church that gladly confesses their desperate need for Him. Because when you really don't know what to do, you ask the One who does.

## PRAYER IS HARD WORK

Can you see again how right theology must lead to right practice? Let's take this moment of spiritual clarity to ask some penetrating questions:

- Does your day start with prayer?
- Does your marriage include prayer?
- Does your quiet time involve prayer?
- Does your leadership prioritize consistent, powerful prayer?
- Does your church leadership actively rely on prayer?

- Do you sneak into your child's bedroom while they're sleeping, get on your knees, and petition the Lord on their behalf?
- Does your church or ministry actively pray for the power, passion, and Spirit of God to promote the glory of God among you?

As I ask these questions, I am reminded of a quote by Robert Murray McCheyne, who said, "You wish to humble a man? Ask him about his prayer life." So we are humbled, yet we are not without hope. We take hold of the right theology of our fantastic need for God and turn to powerful, passionate prayer. We repent of our apathy and self-sufficiency. We repent of our casual and irreverent approach to God. We repent of our prayerlessness and self-righteous reliance, resolved in the truth that today is a new day. We are sobered by the words of E.M. Bounds, who said, "Nothing distinguishes the children of God so clearly and strongly as prayer. It is the one infallible mark and test of being a Christian."[36] To which he adds these sobering words of warning:

> If he [a professed Christian] does not pray, he is a sinner, pure and simple, for prayer is the only way in which the soul of man can enter into fellowship and communion with the source of all Christ-like spirit and energy. Hence, if he prays not, he is not of the household of faith.[37]

It's good if those quotes irritate or convict you somewhat. They should, because the passion and power of prayer has too little place in the heart and lives of most believers and most churches. This cannot be. There is too much at stake and there is no time to lose.

Let us also be abundantly clear on this point: you will not find true, passionate zeal for Christ without prayer to Christ. It is impossible. The problem of prayerlessness is why Jesus told the parable of the persistent widow in Luke 18 that the Church *"ought always to pray and not lose heart"* (Luke 18:1). He decisively and intentionally implored His disciples to pray with tremendous importunity, because this type of shameless prayer reveals a type of heart that eagerly and desperately wants to see the Lord at work in our lives, families, and church. Oh Lord, revive in us a faith that believes in the power of prayer.

## WHY IS PRAYER SO HARD?

But why then is there so little prayer? Why is prayer seemingly so scarce in the majority of believers' lives? Here are a few painful reasons:

**1. Because our flesh opposes prayer.** Prayer is an outright denial to the sinful desires of the flesh. Our sinful flesh loves apathy, laziness, and worldliness. Our sinful flesh constantly tempts us to do the things we don't want to do (Romans 7:20) and opposes the good that we do want to do. Hence, prayer becomes a serious battle with the flesh. Just think of how many times you've thought to yourself, *I should go pray with my wife/kids/friend/neighbour*, but then, almost unexplainably, found yourself in a battle of thought, with one side saying "Do it" and the other saying "Don't do it." This shows us just how powerful prayer really is. Martyn Lloyd-Jones urged, "Always respond to every impulse to pray."[38]

**2. Because Satan hates prayer.** Subtle satanic opposition is why it's so easy to sit down and watch mindless television, but the moment you move towards spiritual momentum in prayer it seems like the distractions of the world come against you at once. In fact, every time you move toward God, expect resistance. As David Eby so brilliantly said about the power of prayer in the face of our enemy:

> What is Satan's attitude toward a church with great programs, a finely tuned organization, a wonderful facility and staff, but with little or no prayer? What is Satan's attitude toward a well-trained, well-educated preacher who prays perfunctorily or little? Satan laughs with a big, belly laugh. He has no fear of this church or this pastor. They are using carnal, worldly weapons in the battle. As they are not full of God-dependence, and full of prayer, they will never challenge the devil's strongholds.
>
> What is Satan's attitude toward a church that earnestly and frequently prays about its worship, preaching, fellowship, evangelism, serving, and about its deeds of love justice and mercy before the watching world? What is his attitude towards a pastor who fervently cries out to God in humility and dependence for Holy Spirit anointing on the preacher's mouth and hearer's ears? No belly laugh. No snickering. Not even a smile. Satan trembles. He knows that a mighty spiritual weapon is being used that will wreak havoc on his strongholds and release his precious captive to his arch-enemy, King Jesus.[39]

Can you see the difference? We're not talking about going through the motions of prayer but entering the arena where prayer is our lifeline. Prayer, along with the sword of the Spirit, is the most powerful weapon we wield (Ephesians 6:10–20). The fully armoured believer who Paul describes in Ephesians 6 is merely protected until he or she wields the Word of God and prayer. We don't counter Satan's attacks with our strength but with reliance on prayer and Scripture, just like Jesus did in Matthew 4:1–11.

Prayer is devastating to the kingdom of darkness because it unleashes God's power. That's why Satan hates authentic prayer so much. What would happen if we would take up our weaponry and mobilize the Church as a whole through simple, dependent, God-empowering prayer? Spiritual mountains would move, that's what would happen.

But again, this is why prayer is such hard work, and all the more reason to dig in and do battle. Once we realize that the strategy of the enemy is to encourage prayerlessness, it should make us all the more fired up and resolved towards prayer-filled lives! As it says in 2 Chronicles 7:14, *"if my people who are called by my name humble themselves, and pray…"*

**3. Because we are tempted to not believe in prayer.** Isn't this true? If we really believed in prayer, we would practice it so much more. As a young believer, I stumbled upon the book by Jim Cymbala called *Fresh Wind, Fresh Fire*. It's a book about prayer and revival, seen through the amazing story of Brooklyn Tabernacle in New York City. I read that book with eagerness and great interest, and after I was finished I closed it and two words came to my mind: prayer works! Honestly, I have never looked at prayer the same way since. It got to the point that within my church as a youth pastor, some called me the "prayer cop." It's only because I was absolutely convinced that if we don't pray, we're dead! Oh how we must believe in prayer and practice it.

**4. Because we don't make time for prayer.** It's hard to do something you don't make time for. It's difficult to pray when it's not even the focal point of the Church. It's almost impossible to gain spiritual momentum towards prayer when the leadership evidently doesn't believe in it. But of course no leader in their right mind would say, "I don't believe in prayer."

The question for those only claiming belief in prayer is this: are you doing it? Enough with the lip service, let's get to the actual application.

## WE ARE CHOSEN FOR PRAYER

Take a look with me at John 15:16 and notice the incredible truth embedded within on the nature of prayer:

> *You did not choose me, but I chose you and appointed you that you should go and bear fruit and that your fruit should abide, s*o that whatever you ask the Father in my name, *he may give it to you.* (emphasis added)

Notice the biblical truth and pattern of our salvation in Christ. The Lord Jesus chose us in order to bear fruit *through* us and to hear prayer *from* us. Do you see that? His choosing of us must result in prayer from us. Prayer is so vital for the Christian life that it should be as natural as breathing. This is wonderfully challenging and inspiring to me; I have been chosen for prayer! The people of God have been separated by God for prayer to God, resulting in the glory of God.

Just think about it: an individual or church that doesn't have prayer at its core is like a shiny vehicle without an engine. Yes, you can admire how pretty and attractive this vehicle is, you can admire its cool gadgets and features, but when you pop the hood, you'll discover there is nothing inside to make it run. Just think of all the ministries that obsess with looking shiny yet deny the engine altogether. We can never become that church or person who's trying to run without an engine. The moment we do, we're of no use to the Lord Jesus Christ.

The significance of prayer is proof of the reality check that will take place at the judgment of believers (2 Corinthians 5:10). When that moment comes, we will find out just what the Lord truly valued and honoured. Many a leader and ministry will be utterly shocked at what ended up as hay and what ended up gold (1 Corinthians 3:11–14). This is why the starting point of our own passion must be the decision to imitate the passions of Jesus Christ; He prayed without ceasing. Considering that Jesus said we were chosen for prayer, I like the idea of putting our eggs in the basket of prayer. You simply cannot lose, ever.

Remember, a prayerless life is a life that fundamentally declares, "I don't need you, God." But a prayer-filled life is a life consistently saying, "Help me, oh God." By the grace of God, I choose the latter.

Please allow me to close this chapter practicing on your behalf what I've been preaching:

Oh Father, renew our minds as to the true and beautiful theology of prayer. Oh Father, would that Your children recognize their infinite need and respond with sincere humility in crying out to You day and night. Revive Your Church in dependence on and in desperation for Your power. May we be ever aware of our pathetic self-sufficiency and therefore drawn to Your perfect sufficiency. May we call out as one that unless You go with us, we will not move forward. May we gladly declare our inability and inadequacy, but then revel and marvel in You, the God of all glory and power. Please, oh Lord, give us a heart of prayer. We pray that we would be a people of prayer, longing, loving, and leaning into Your grace through passionate and powerful prayer. In Jesus' name, amen.

**FOR FURTHER THOUGHT AND REFLECTION**

A little while ago, my wife Gill and I visited the Billy Graham Library in Charlotte, North Carolina. We took the "journey of faith" dedicated to the life of Billy Graham, a powerful experience. As we walked through the audio and visual evidence of the massive impact of Billy Graham's ministry, we came across several amazing quotes from this faithful servant of God. Here is one of them. What do these words tell you about the secret of both humility and prayer in the Christian life?

The secret is not me. So many people think that somehow I carry a revival around in my suitcase, and they just announce me and something happens, but that's not true. This is the work of God, and the Bible warns that God will not share His glory with another. All the publicity that we receive sometimes frightens me because I feel that therein lies a great danger. If God should take His hand off me, I would have no more spiritual power. The whole secret of the success of our meetings is spiritual, it's God answering prayer. I cannot take credit for any of it.

## CHAPTER NINE
The Clarity of Passion: Simplicity

*One thing have I asked of the Lord, that will I seek after:*
*that I may dwell in the house of the Lord all the days of*
*my life, to gaze upon the beauty of the Lord and to inquire*
*in his temple.*

—Psalm 27:4

To have what we want is riches, but to be able to do
without is power.[40]

—George MacDonald

The irony amazes me. Never before have we lived in such
a technologically rich generation that invents ways to
make our lives easier and increase our pleasure and leisure. Yet
with all this convenience, we see a new generation that, in my
opinion, has never been more distracted and preoccupied. In
our apparent pursuit of simplicity, life has become increasingly
complicated, rushed, and frantic. If we are going to have any
hope of true passion for Christ, the chaos must stop. It must.

Take a moment and examine the pursuits of your heart.
What calls for your attention? What motivates you? What fires

up your affections? Do your true passions lean towards the temporal or the eternal?

- How much time do you spend with your smartphone? There's probably an app that will give you that number to the minute. Do you control it or does it control you?
- How much time do you spend entertaining yourself with internet, video games, sports, hobbies, TV, and movies?
- How much affection do you invest towards money, possessions, and sex?
- What causes your heart to truly be filled with affection? Shopping? Golf? Vacation? Be honest.
- How much mental energy do you expend planning your next material purchase?

Here's the bottom line: pursuit of the temporal pours water on our fires for Christ, but eternal pursuits stoke our fires for Christ. The most dangerous part of pursuing the idolatry of the world is that in the end we become what we worship. I'll say it again: we become what we worship. Scary!

Psalm 115:4–8 states the danger so pointedly:

*Their idols are silver and gold, the work of human hands. They have mouths, but do not speak; eyes, but do not see. They have ears, but do not hear; noses, but do not smell. They have hands, but do not feel; feet, but do not walk; and they do not make a sound in their throat.* Those who make them become like them; so do all who trust in them. (emphasis added)

I emphasized the final sentence because it's the most important. Those who make idols become like idols—but hear this: so do all who trust in them.

The response I often get when I suggest we're in danger of trusting idols is, "What? Me? I don't trust in idols. No way." But the starting point for this conversation is understanding what John Calvin said: "Man's nature, so to speak, is a perpetual factory of idols."[41] The best question isn't "Do I have any idols?" but "Where and what are my idols?" This question marks a person of wisdom and humility. We must assume that our hearts are always at risk of idolatry, because the possibilities of distraction are seemingly endless. How many individuals, families, and churches have I seen grow lukewarm due to a creeping shift toward idolatrous distractions? Too many!

## MY LIFE DOES NOT CONSIST IN THE ABUNDANCE OF MY POSSESSIONS

Part of my salvation story involved the Word of God becoming alive and a treasure to my soul. I remember well a passage that changed my entire perspective on life; the insight it gave me was thrilling, freeing, and so powerful. For the first twenty-two years of my life, I was indoctrinated into the system of the world, which convinced me that my life *did* consist in the abundance of my possessions.

I was taught through high school, and particularly university, that my identity was in my success, my career, my ability to purchase, and ultimately my possessions. I was constantly striving and longing for the material. I was desperately grasping at more and working hard to get more. I constantly competed with others, wanting to outdo them to prove that I had more, a boost to my self-esteem and self-worth. How sad, but how true.

Then I stumbled onto Luke 12:15: *"Take care, and be on your guard against all covetousness, for one's life does not consist in the abundance of his possessions."*

I distinctly remember how I felt when I first read this text with a regenerated heart and a renewed mind. It was yet another moment of my blinders being lifted, of the chains being broken off and hurled into the depths of the sea. With that verse, I experienced truth, stunning clarity, and the shock of the sword of the Spirit slicing through the lies of the prince of the power of the air (Ephesians 2).

Frankly, the effect of God's Word was exhilarating. But why was this challenge from Jesus such a big deal? Because for the first time in my life I knew and believed that my life did *not* consist in the abundance of my possessions. My spirit leapt within me. All the striving, all the envy, all the jealousy, all the useless toil, all the self-made effort to try and become something or someone that seemed impossible, all of that was done. In the space of a few seconds, none of the obsessions of our world or its fanatical idolatry mattered anymore.

Now I could answer with confidence another of Jesus' life-altering questions: *"For what does it profit a man if he gains the whole world and loses or forfeits himself?"* (Luke 9:25) I could shout: "Nothing!" Every promise the world had put before me was a distraction from the truth that a life outside of God's purposes would put me on a wide road to eternity apart from Him.

Oh how powerful the light is when it truly shines upon our hearts. How glorious and freeing it is to see and believe the words of our Lord Jesus Christ. I found the power to stare down the demonic system of our world and say, "I don't need you and I am not you." By the grace of God, I was granted the clarity and simplicity to understand that my worth and value was contained in the Lord Jesus Christ. It didn't matter what others thought, how much I owned, or what I had achieved, because in reality I had *everything*.

This life-transforming realization is the power of the gospel, and it produces a God-glorifying and Christ-exalting passion in our hearts. Imagine truly being freed from the distraction and idolatry of obsessively pursuing more stuff. Admit right now that this has ruled your heart for too long and in too many ways. Face the reality that you are tempted so often to place your worth in what you own or possess. Instead, here's the truth worth shouting from the rooftop: "My life does not consist in the abundance of my possessions!" What a joy! What a freedom! What a truth!

## MR. & MRS. THING

Several years ago, I came across this very insightful anecdote of Mr. and Mrs. Thing:[42]

> Mr. and Mrs. Thing are a very pleasant and successful couple, at least that's the verdict of most people who tend to measure success with a thingometer. When the thingometer is put to work in the life of Mr. and Mrs. Thing, the result is startling. There he is, sitting down on a very luxurious and expensive thing, almost hidden by a large number of other things. Things to sit on, things to sit at, things to cook on, things to eat from. All shiny and new. Things, things, things. Things to clean with, things to wash with, things to clean and things to wash. Things to amuse, things to give pleasure, things to watch, and things to play. Things for the long, hot summer and things for the short, cold winter. Things for the big thing in which they live, and things for the

garden, and things for the lounge, and things for the kitchen, and things for the bedroom. And things on four wheels, things on two wheels, and things to put on top of the things on four wheels, and things to pull behind the four wheels, and things to add to the interior of the thing on four wheels. Things, things, things , and there in the middle are Mr. and Mrs. Thing, smiling, pleased as pink with their things, thinking of more things to add to their things, secure in their castle of things.

Well, I just want you to know that your things can't last. They're going to pass. There's going to be an end to them. Maybe an error in judgment, maybe a temporary loss of concentration, or maybe you'll just pass them off to the second-hand thing dealer. Or maybe they'll wind up a mass of mangled metal being towed off to the thing yard. And what about all the things in your house? Well, it's time for bed. Put out the cat. Make sure you lock the door to make sure some thing-taker doesn't come and take your things. And that's the way life goes, doesn't it? And someday when you die, they only put one thing in the box. You.

How well can you relate to Mr. and Mrs. Thing? For the love of God, let us not be taken over by "things." Seriously, for the love of God.

In Psalm 52, David pushes the seriousness of this truth even further when he says, *"See the man who would not make God his refuge, but trusted in the abundance of his riches and sought refuge in his own destruction!"* (Psalm 52:7, emphasis added) It's hard to miss the devastation of trusting in things that *"moth and rust destroy"* (Matthew 6:19). The tragedy is that the person who trusts in such things gets destroyed also. Wow!

## YOU CAN HAVE THE WORLD, JUST GIVE ME JESUS

I am convinced that one of the leading causes, if not *the* cause, of apathy in the Western Church is a divided and diluted devotion due to materialism. The longing for wealth, riches, and things is ripping out from within us a genuine and passionate pursuit of Jesus Christ. Psalm 16:4 says, *"The sorrows of those who run after another god shall multiply."* The treasuring and gathering up of wealth and possessions doesn't multiply joy; in the end it will multiply sorrows.

In the story of the rich man and Lazarus found in Luke 16:19–31, the rich man spent his life as one of the rich and famous, feasting sumptuously and wearing the best clothes, but in the end he found himself in the torment of Hades, wishing that he could have one drop of water to cool his tongue. Wake up, generation! Wake up to the realities of life and the realities of death! We are being called to life in Christ, treasures in Christ, and passion for Christ. Now is the time to *"[wake] up from your drunken stupor, as is right, and do not go on sinning"* (1 Corinthians 15:34). Now is the time!

Furthermore, the way we think must change from the root. We have been deceived into believing a monstrous lie about power. The quote from George MacDonald that began this chapter is so perceptive: "To have what we want is riches, but to be able to do without is power."[43] Simple singlemindedness is the secret power that the apostle Paul summarized in these words: *"For to me to live is Christ, and to die is gain"* (Philippians 1:21). He knew the simplicity of devotion to Jesus, which we are called to know as well. And just in case we miss the point, Paul added,

*Indeed, I count everything as loss because of the surpassing worth of knowing Christ Jesus my Lord. For his sake I have*

*suffered the loss of all things and count them as rubbish, in
order that I may gain Christ...* (Philippians 3:8)

This focus will absolutely lead to passion for Christ.
Progress in clarity is when you realize that earthly treasures
simply cannot fulfill and will never satisfy.

Look at yet another instruction from God's Word
regarding this truth about the few things that actually matter
for eternity:

*Be not afraid when a man becomes rich, when the glory of
his house increases. For when he dies he will carry nothing
away; his glory will not go down after him. For though,
while he lives, he counts himself blessed—and though you
get praise when you do well for yourself—his soul will go
to the generation of his fathers, who will never again see
light.* (Psalm 49:16–19)

What a glorious moment it is when you realize, believe,
and act upon the truth that Jesus Christ is the only One who
satisfies. This is when simplicity becomes so radiant, beautiful,
and attractive. This is the call for our lives right now, the
call for passion in the glory of Jesus Christ. The clarity of
complete commitment to Christ causes one's life to simplify
and supernaturally organize. This is when the cluttered, frantic,
anxiety-filled, and stress-saturated live ceases. The grip of stress
loosens, causing us to smile with relief and joy.

Jesus wants to give us the ability to see what is of true value
and lead our lives according to these truths. Only His beauty
is worthy of our true passion. When we finally see that our
value comes from the gospel of Jesus Christ and our identity
rests in the inheritance of Jesus Christ, we can say in our lives

with power and boldness, "I'm done with this empty pursuit of things. My resolve is for my Saviour."

Remember, you will never stare in the face of Jesus Christ and feel disappointed. Never! There will never be a single time in your existence when you behold the face of your Saviour and feel either let down or dissatisfied. It's impossible, because He is perfect. This is why David in Psalm 27 said,

> *One thing have I asked of the Lord, that I will seek after: that I may dwell in the house of the Lord all the days of my life, to gaze upon the beauty of the Lord and inquire in his temple.* (Psalm 27:4)

Notice that David asked only one thing. Now that's glorious simplicity. One thing will I seek after… the beauty and glory of Jesus Christ.

## SIMPLICITY PROMOTES PASSION

This call for simplicity results in a life-changing passion. Do you believe it? Do you have it? Regardless of where you've been, you can have that passion. If you start to believe by faith that Jesus Christ is truly your all, your satisfaction, and your joy, the living water will trickle down into your soul. Soon this water will turn into a stream, and then a river. As you truly pursue and seek Him, you will find Him (Jeremiah 29:13), and you will not be disappointed. Then you will be able to join with the psalmist to say, *"You have put more joy in my heart than they have when their grain and wine abound"* (Psalm 4:7). Yes, Lord, may it be so!

May there be a growing conviction and resolve within you to passionately pursue Jesus Christ. May you be free to declare out loud and know deep in your heart that Jesus Christ is the source of all true joy and your true treasure. And here is what is so exciting and guaranteed: when this happens, it will make the world taste and seem like garbage (Philippians 3:8). Really, it will.

Please oh Lord, hear our prayer and move us towards a Spirit-filled simplicity that will revolutionize our minds, affections, and wills.

## STEPS TO SIMPLICITY

So what are some practical steps you can take towards simplicity in order to strengthen your passion for Christ?

**1. Contentment.** As we've discussed earlier, spiritual contentment is bad, but material contentment is good. Material contentment is the ability to stare the world in the face and say "I'm good." As in "No thanks, I'm full." The apostle Paul said, *"Not that I am speaking of being in need, for I have learned in whatever situation I am to be content"* (Philippians 4:11). It is so powerful in this life to know and feel contentment. I love when I can stare down yet another commercial telling me my life is incomplete without their product and say, "That's a lie and I am content." The amazing part is that the more we are filled with passion *for* Christ, the more we are satisfied *in* Christ. And the more we are satisfied in Christ, the more contentment we experience in this life. It is truly a beautiful and powerful place to be.

**2. Generosity.** With simplicity comes generosity. Because we simply need less, we are able to give more. This is a hallmark of the genuine Christian life. Open-handedness— do you have it? I have yet to find in Scripture or meet in person a stingy, miserly, or tight-fisted person with a genuine passion for Christ. And why is that? Because all their passion is tied up in their obsession with holding on to their material stuff. The same could be said about an individual motivated by greed. They don't have room for passion for Christ; it's all taken up with self.

This is why simplicity is an undervalued discipline; it can unleash generosity from our lives. If you truly follow Christ, you must also be generous. After all, *"[for] you know the grace of our Lord Jesus Christ, that though he was rich, yet for your sake he became poor, so that you by his poverty might become rich"* (2 Corinthians 8:9). The life of Jesus was the greatest example of generosity ever. We will find tremendous freedom, power, and joy through our lives as we believe in simplicity and move towards generosity. Generosity is the overflow of the gospel in our lives. If we get it, we give.

**3. Tenacity.** What I mean by this is that Christ gives us a growing determination to rid ourselves of idolatry. Search your heart and life to find out what has a hold on you. Join me in going through a weekly examination I call an "idol search." When I see invitations to shift my passion, I seek to kill them. It's a painful yet life-giving process that keeps the fire burning for my Saviour.

For some of you, you need to literally smash something idolatrous or get rid of it altogether. You need to be tenacious in taking action toward simplicity for the sake of Christ in your life. It's startling to see the tenacity of our world, often including believers, when it comes to the accumulation of material overabundance. If only we would exercise the same tenacity towards the care of our souls. After all, Jesus did not come to give abundant wealth, but abundant life (John 10:10).

**4. Gratitude.** Choose thankfulness right now. How powerful and simple it is to be thankful to the Lord in all things (Philippians 4:6; 1 Thessalonians 5:18). Gratitude destroys complaining about what you lack and lusting after what you don't have. Choose right now to look around and recognize all that you've been given by the Lord. I recommend starting with His salvation in your life. Speak out loud all that you recognize as His grace and keep going until you sense His peace flow into your heart and life.

It's amazing how powerful this discipline is and how it causes us to rejoice in His grace, goodness, and generosity towards us. This powerful aspect of simplicity changes us on an everyday basis. Remember, it's almost impossible to be grumpy and grateful at the same time. Choose gratitude.

## A FINAL WORD: CONVICTION, NOT CONDEMNATION

If you're feeling convicted from these last pages, join the club. Allow me to reinforce the gospel. The Lord loves you; He absolutely and perfectly loves you. His grace overcomes all your sin and all your failure, *all* of it! The intention of this teaching is not to produce guilt, but to produce conviction. The enemy will try and turn this into condemnation, but we know there is no condemnation for those in Christ Jesus (Romans 8:1).

However, the Holy Spirit will bring conviction. After all, this is one of His great purposes and roles (John 16:8). So we shake off guilt, but we do invite conviction, all the while knowing we are absolutely covered in the grace of God. God's grace, in His love for us, refuses to allow us to stay in mediocrity and apathy. His grace and love pursue us and woo us back to Himself. His grace and inexhaustible, unchanging love will not let us settle in complacency. Don't you see, His grace is calling you to change right now. His grace is calling your name to greater heights in Him.

Grace is an important word right now, especially for those who tend towards attitudes of legalism. Be released in the grace of the Lord and respond to His love, His wonderful, awesome love that will not allow you to remain as you are. He simply loves you too much to let you stay as you are, and that's why He has brought you this message at this time in your life. He calls you in grace to more and more of Him.

## FURTHER THOUGHT AND REFLECTION

- Take time to go over the above steps to simplicity again. In what specific areas is the Holy Spirit bringing you conviction? What steps can you take this week to see a difference?
- In this chapter, we read that the pursuit of the temporal pours water on our fires for Christ. Can you see how your passion for Christ has been hindered by idolatrous pursuits?
- It takes faith to believe and live out the reality that the Lord Jesus is more satisfying than the world. Do you truly believe this through the actions of your life?
- What specific hobby or desire needs to be put in proper perspective today? How can this be diminished so that Christ can be exalted?

**CHAPTER TEN**
The Harvest of Passion: Souls

*...for I have appeared to you for this purpose... to open their eyes, so that they may turn from darkness to light and from the power of Satan to God, that they may receive forgiveness of sins and a place among those who are sanctified by faith in me..*

—Acts 26:16, 18

You do not love the Lord at all unless you love the souls of others.[44]

—Charles Spurgeon

I didn't want to go into ministry. I also confess that my wife didn't want to marry a pastor. But here we are, all these years later, and we wouldn't trade the life God has given us for anything. Sure, I've wanted to quit dozens of times (really, I have), but the call to preach life change for the glory of God spurs me on over and over again.

Not too long after my conversion, I began to sense a nudging from the Holy Spirit toward ministry. However, my faulty idea of ministry was something I wasn't at all interested in. So in response to God's hints, I proceeded to move in the opposite direction. I quickly found out that God tends to win—actually, He always wins—and although I tried to be Jonah, it wasn't long until I found myself in the ocean, inside the fish, ready to give in to the will of God.

When I realized that I didn't have a choice and that God's calling was heavy upon me, I put up a sort of fleece to the Lord. I remember saying, "Lord, if we're going to do this (ministry), let's see some lives changed for Your glory." Because I was so acutely aware of God's absolute transforming power upon my life, I was struck by the potential of His glory in everyone's life. That awareness became the ambition for His glory through changed lives. I increasingly found myself with a tremendous appetite for salvation and sanctification. I lived to see people's lives turned upside-down in the beauty of grace and the glory of God.

All these years later, one of my favourite moments of worship is our church's baptism services. How incredible it is to hear person after person testify to the fact that they were blind, but now they see; they were lost, but are now found; they were dead, but are now alive! What is more glorious than seeing a person spiritually raised from the dead (2 Corinthians 5:17), proclaiming the glory of God? A passion for God will *always* lead to a passion for souls. Do you have a passion for souls? We must.

## FROM THE POWER OF SATAN TO GOD

In Acts 26, the apostle Paul found himself sharing his testimony before King Agrippa II. In the presence of an earthly king, Paul revealed the extraordinary purpose and pursuit of his life: a passion for souls. As he explained the outworking of his conversion in the gospel, he recalled what Jesus had said to him:

*"But rise and stand upon your feet, for I have appeared to you for this purpose…"* (Acts 26:16)

This statement really gets my attention, especially the word "purpose." Jesus is detailing His plans for the life of Paul, the passion for souls for the glory of God. Paul was describing his former way of life as a persecutor of the Church. The apostle revealed to Agrippa that before meeting Jesus he had thought he knew the purpose of his life and had been completely focused on carrying it out, even though it happened to be opposite to the will of God. What Jesus told him on the road to Damascus was "Your purpose is gone, but my purpose has arrived." Awesome.

I also get fired up about the words *"rise and stand upon your feet."* In other words, there's no time for laziness or inaction; there's simply too much to do for the gospel and for God's glory. Jesus said, essentially, "C'mon, Paul, let's get after it. There are souls to be won for the glory of God." Now that's a word the Church needs to hear in our day.

And look at what comes next in this text: *"…for I have appeared to you for this purpose, to appoint you as a servant and witness to the things in which you have seen…"* (Acts 26:16) The verb "to appoint" is significant because it includes the sense of beforehand, meaning that the announcement of Paul's appointment came long after the actual commission. Jesus was indicating that Paul had been set apart before his birth to carry out the task of preaching the gospel. Paul was appointed to be a *"servant and a witness."* He was to be a witness of the resurrected Christ, and a servant for the proclamation of the gospel to the Gentiles.

Notice the end of Acts 26:17: *"to whom I am sending you…"* Jesus had a passion for souls and He was sending out Paul with the same passion. Paul had just received the greatest purpose and privilege known to humans. There is no higher calling than the proclamation of the gospel of Jesus Christ. It's the message of life. This wasn't only Paul's calling, but all of our callings. Jesus, in the Great Commission, made it abundantly clear that the passion for souls is not just for a select few, but to be seen across His entire Church. Oh may it be so!

Can you recall the period of your life when you were transformed by the grace of the gospel? Can you remember that moment when Jesus intervened directly into your self-led, self-driven purpose and changed your heart? Can you recollect how light from heaven shone into your soul and changed your life forever? This was when Jesus presented His authority, grace, and purpose for your life. This was when Jesus stepped in and said, "Your purpose is gone and my purpose has arrived."

For every genuine believer in Jesus Christ, this is your story and current situation. You and I are now living for the purpose of the glory of Jesus Christ in the proclamation of the gospel. Just as Paul was appointed to be a servant and a witness, we too have been appointed to the same. We have been set apart by the Lord to be witnesses and servants of the gospel of Jesus Christ. This has been verified and proven through the Great Commission in Matthew 28:18–20.

So this was Paul's purpose, but what was his motivation? He answers this question in Acts 26:18:

> ...to open their eyes, so that they may turn from darkness to light and from the power of Satan to God, that they may receive forgiveness of sins and a place among those who are sanctified by faith in me.

Wow! Read that verse again. This is why you and I are called to passion for God, and then a passion for souls—because lives are at stake! We are to help people turn from darkness to light, from the power of Satan to God, to see them receive forgiveness and a place among those sanctified by faith in Jesus. Incredible! No wonder Charles Spurgeon said, "You do not love the Lord at all unless you love the souls of others."[45] You can't separate these two things. They always go together. Always.

The only point I would add to Spurgeon's thought is that you can't love others without loving the Lord. The one affects the other, but they always go together. That is exactly why the first and second greatest commandments are to love God and then love others (Matthew 22:37–39). A true passion for Christ leads necessarily to a true passion for souls.

## THE BOOKENDS OF THE GREAT COMMISSION
Even with the calling to have a passion for souls ringing in our ears, many believers are hesitant to live out and speak their faith due to fear of rejection. We will acknowledge the Great Commission with our minds, but our hearts trail behind.

This fear is addressed when we see and understand the bookends of the Great Commission. So often we recall Matthew 28:19–20, but we forget the all-essential truth that surrounds this commission in verses 18 and 20. These two truths change everything! The bookends of the Great Commission include the *power* of Jesus and the promised *presence* of Jesus.

In Matthew 28:18–19, Jesus says, *"All authority in heaven and on earth has been given to me. Go therefore…"* Did you see that empowerment? Notice the phrase *"all authority"* just before the command *"Go therefore."* The whole premise of the Commission for the bride of Christ is founded on the authority of Jesus Christ Himself. He states right here that all authority has been given to Him. Not *some* authority or *most* of the authority, but all of the authority. Does this not change everything regarding who is actually empowering the call and passion for souls within our lives?

Jesus was simply exercising His authority when He said in Matthew 16:18, *"I will build my church, and the gates of hell shall not prevail against it."* He can say this because He can't be stopped, ever. He is sovereign; He is ruler; He is Lord of all. What He decides happens and what He says goes. Jesus' awesome position as the Second Person in the Trinity is why the "therefore" in the Great Commission carries such massive weight—because it's built upon the truth of where all authority and power comes from. So we don't advance on the mission to see souls saved by relying on our own strength or effort or authority. No way. That is a futile effort. However, when we realize that we carry the authority of the Lord of the universe, our faith and boldness changes.

But there's another significant bookend to the Great Commission. The very end of Matthew 28:20 says this, *"And behold, I am with you always, to the end of the age."* If the first bookend was the *power* of Christ, the second is the guaranteed *presence* of Christ. This is utterly essential, because it allows us to realize how a passion for souls is developed—not by our doing, but by the promised presence of Christ Himself. This verse has been used to carry missionaries to the ends of the earth with a boldness and joy that can only be described as supernatural.

John Piper, in his excellent series entitled The Swans Are Not Silent,[46] includes a biography of John G. Paton which is sure to inspire even the dullest of heart towards Christ. It was John Paton who took hold of the promise of *"And behold, I am with you always, even to the end of the age,"* which allowed him to endure the most extreme pressure of missionary life. Paton was surrounded by crisis, trial, severe danger, and heartache throughout his life. Despite repeated setbacks and opposition, he gave his entire life to the cause of the gospel, in the passion of souls, rooted in the promise of the power and presence of his Saviour. Wow! John Piper says about Paton that "more than any other promise, this one brought Jesus close and real to John Paton in all his dangers."[47] Here's what Paton himself said regarding this unchanging truth:

> Without the abiding consciousness of the presence and power of my dear Lord and Saviour, nothing else in all the world could have preserved me from losing my reason and perishing miserably. In His words, "Lo, I am with you always, even unto the end of the world," became to me so real that it would not have startled me to behold Him, as Stephen did, gazing down upon the scene. I felt His supporting power… It is the sober truth, and it comes back to me sweetly after twenty years, that I had my nearest and dearest glimpses of the face and smiles of my blessed Lord in those dread moments when musket, club, or spear was being levelled at my life. Oh the bliss of living and enduring, as seeing "Him who is invisible"![48]

Notice that glorious final line. The bliss that is found when we truly see, when we recognize the presence of the One who is invisible. The instant comfort, joy, and boldness it brings to our hearts to press on and testify without regrets to the glory and grace that is alone found in Jesus Christ the Lord. Again, *"And behold, I am with you always, even to the end of the age."*

This verse has brought comfort to the direst of situations, has inspired faith in the most persecuted of churches, and grants courage to the weakest of saints. It's a guarantee that grants passion and boldness for souls—because it's not from us, it's from Him.

You see, this is the grace of God. We ultimately cannot produce a true passion for souls or a saving of souls. However, we are called to see the passion, power, and presence of Christ in the pursuit of souls, and then join Him.

This view of our calling changes everything. We are not alone; we have Christ with us. We don't speak on our own authority; we speak on the authority of Christ. We don't produce fruit or change lives; we plant and water, but only God gives the growth (1 Corinthians 3:6). Don't you see how this truth creates more passion for the souls of others, because of the promises we have about His power and presence? Our confidence is bolstered because of the truth that it is not up to us or even about us, not at all. Praise the Lord that it is not about us, and that's what fuels us to step out, speak out, and be sold out for our Saviour.

Thank the Lord for the bookends of the Great Commission. Without them we don't stand a chance, but with them we simply cannot lose!

## CULTIVATING A PASSION FOR SOULS

I love our church's evangelism strategy. It's so simple and so clear. Our evangelism strategy is our people. I always say to our newcomers group, "Our evangelism strategy is you, it's me; it's us." What I mean is that I firmly believe that if you're living out what Jesus has done and is doing in your life with sincerity and passion, you can't help but desire to share the message of Christ with others.

I always tell our people, "The Holy Spirit is never—I repeat, never—saying to you, 'Ssshhhhh, don't talk about Jesus, we're ashamed!' The Holy Spirit will never do that." The Holy Spirit rejoices to speak of the risen and glorious Saviour. It is the Holy Spirit who fills us and grants us boldness to speak the message of salvation to a lost and dying world. I am convinced, because I have seen it over and over again, that a person who is filled with love for the Lord, broken before Him, grounded in His truth, and dependent in prayer will also desire to speak and share about Jesus Christ. It really is that simple.

Do we train people how to evangelize in our church? Yes, of course, but it's passion for the Lord and conviction of the gospel that cannot be contained within so many of our people. Why? Because when you're deeply aware of the truth that saves you from death and has given you life, you can't stop the urgency, love, and passion from flowing over.

As a pastor, I see weekly evidence that we have people witnessing and bringing people to church. So many of our people are filled with love for the lost because that's Christ working in them. And this witnessing isn't a watered-down, half version of the gospel, but a real and authentic call to the truth of Jesus Christ. These results happen because where there's a true passion for Christ, there must be a true passion for souls. Again, do you have it? Do you have passion for Christ and a passion for souls?

No wonder so many believers and churches are lacking life change and passion for the lost. Fundamentally, they lack a true passion for Christ, and changing this condition must begin with the leadership of the church. If passion for Christ is not burning at the top, it's unlikely to reach the rest for Christ. There might be a few burning with zeal, but the fire will be difficult and frustrating to keep going in the midst of apathy, fear, and lukewarm living.

Pastors, elders, and leaders who are reading this, take an honest inventory of your life. Where's your heart? What's the condition of your passion for Christ? Where are your convictions on display? Remember, you can't teach what you don't know, and you can't lead where you won't go.

## PERMISSION TO BE BOLD

I remember so well the first day I met James MacDonald, pastor of Harvest Bible Chapel in Chicago. I was a young man and part of a good church, but one that may have been held back by a fear of man opposed to the fear of God. We weren't pursuing bad things, but not the best things. There was such a concern for the care of man that it actually led to a fear of man. At the time, I was only vaguely aware that something didn't seem right.

Now I understand that wherever there's a fear of man, there will be a lack of fear of God. Let us be very careful in our day to remember that the Bible tells us that the *fear of the Lord is the beginning of wisdom…* " (Proverbs 9:10) The simple biblical math is that if you remove the fear of the Lord, you also take out the wisdom of God. Doesn't that explain a lot of church culture and ineffectiveness in our day? No wonder entire denominations are lying in rubble. If you remove a deep reverence and passion for the Lord and His Word, you essentially remove God from the church. And if you remove God from the church, I don't like your chances.

On the day I met James MacDonald, I was in a place of restlessness, and quite honestly I was tempted towards deep discouragement. I was searching for a vision of leadership that was of God, not man. I know that sounds odd, yet I know so many are in the same place, where the human and man-centred has replaced the Christ-centred in our minds, and therefore our hearts.

When James MacDonald walked into the room, I heard for the first time in my life a clear, passionate, conviction-filled, Christ-centred, and boldness-driven vision for the Church.

Pastor James expressed without reservation his passion for Christ, his confidence in the authority of the Word, his deep love for the Church, and His burning desire for the glory of God alone. He spoke with an urgency, clarity, and transparency that was foreign to me yet directly connected with my restlessness.

Coming from the environment I was part of, I honestly didn't know you could even talk this way. That day, in a way I cannot fully explain, a fire of vision and leadership was lit, confirmed, and has yet to go out. I am convinced that the well-intentioned yet man-centred tendencies of the leadership around me was diminishing my passion for Christ. But the Lord in His grace sent a prophet of truth to free me to pursue Him, releasing me to a path of boldness in the passion of souls. I truly believe that this day was given to me by the Lord to grant me permission to be bold. I wonder how many reading this even now are also stuck in the fear of man and need a new vision of the Lord. Do you need to receive permission to be bold? Consider yourself permitted!

2 Timothy 1:7 says that *"God gave us a spirit not of fear but of power and love and self-control."* Many believers are familiar with this verse, but what about the very next one? 2 Timothy 1:8 adds, *"Therefore do not be ashamed of the testimony about our Lord…"* No wonder Paul said in Romans 1:16, *"For I am not ashamed of the gospel, for it is the power of God for salvation…"*

Sit still right now, wherever you are, in the quiet of the moment, and hear the voice of God from His Word saying to you, "I give you permission to be bold." Oh may it be so! A permission to be bold in the passion of souls.

## THE DAYS ARE EVIL

I'm not sure about you, but I don't need any more evidence from our world that the days are evil and that the day of judgment is drawing near. I'm not making predictions; I'm reading the signs. I am convinced that if there's ever a time to live with urgency for Christ, this is it. I mean, how much more evidence do we need that the world will not satisfy and the ways of man simply will not do? How much more hurt, pain, violence, disasters, and flat-out evil do we need to see to stop living for the earth and start living with passion for Jesus Christ? Ephesians 5:15–17 makes it very clear:

> *Look carefully then how you walk, not as unwise but as wise, making the best use of the time, because the days are evil. Therefore do not be foolish, but understand what the will of the Lord is.*

Let us wake up and look around. The days are evil! But this doesn't mean we run and hide. No way. I believe this is the exact time to live with passion for Christ and His glory. We can all see so clearly what actually lasts and has meaning. All around us is the evidence of futile attempts of living for materialism, earthly riches, and self-consumed pleasures. It's all for not, for the world is so uncertain. That's exactly why we live for the One who is perfect, sovereign, and immutable.

Now more than ever, the world's condition is the reason we must have a passion for souls. D.L. Moody said, "I would rather save one soul from death than have a monument of solid gold reaching from my grave to the heavens."[49] Wow! I guess we know why he was so powerfully used. He had a passion for souls.

Understand that once the passion starts flowing from the top, it becomes a tremendous force in our lives. What starts with a love for Christ and a brokenness before Him begins to form into a river. In many ways, once the river gets going it is a powerful force, difficult to stop.

Lord, may it be so in many people and churches. May the tide of true passion overwhelm a growing number of believers. May these simple truths fill us with faith, hope, and love. Oh God, may we begin to have true passion for you that leads to a true passion for souls.

Believe me, when you have a true passion for souls, you will start to see a true passion for *revival*.

## FURTHER THOUGHT AND REFLECTION:

- How does Charles Spurgeon's quote—"You do not love the Lord at all unless you love the souls of others"—impact you? Have you thought about it in this way before?
- How do the bookends of the Great Commission (power and presence) inspire and encourage you to long for souls more often?
- In what ways are you able to see how a lack of fear of the Lord can be so devastating to our individual lives and the Church?
- What truth from this chapter will you hold onto at all costs, faced with the reality that our days are evil?

## CHAPTER ELEVEN
The Longing of Passion: Revival

*Will you not revive us again, that your people may rejoice in you?*

—Psalm 85:6

The only reason we don't have revival is because we are willing to live without it.[50]

—Leonard Ravenhill

A chapter on revival is the only fitting conclusion to a book pleading with God's people to be infused with God's passion. When we understand and apply the gospel to every part of our lives, we truly behold the treasure gifted to us at the cross and cannot stop our zeal for God. And when we approach God with this kind of heart-bursting passion, when God's people take up His purposes for them in the pursuit of Him, when the Church begins to truly seek Him, worship Him, pray to Him, and love Him, God responds.

*...if my people who are called by my name humble themselves, and pray and seek my face and turn from*

*their wicked ways, then I will hear from heaven and will forgive their sin and heal their land.* (2 Chronicles 7:14)

At this point, the cynics will undoubtedly say, "Our world is way too evil for revival to reach our land." I understand that objection, and many times I am tempted to fall into the same line of thinking.

However, when I read the biography of George Whitefield, where massive revival broke out in his lifetime and through his ministry, I noticed something significant about his environment. The obvious intent of the book's introduction is to prove the depths of evil in the society that surrounded George Whitefield. The author compared the society of the eighteenth century with that of our current day and suggested that conditions were probably worse in Whitefield's day than they are now. He really wanted to dispel this notion that revival is not possible in our day by demonstrating that the very same thing could have been said in the eighteenth century. But it was into that very time that God descended upon the land and brought about one of the greatest revivals in history.

I must admit that as I read this, I felt both rebuked and incredibly encouraged. The author is right. We can't limit what God can do, ever. Why not revival in our day? Why not pray and ask and seek the Lord for greater and greater things? Why not desire that more lives be changed for the glory of God? Why not petition our God for a passion in the Church that has not been seen in decades? Why not beg Him for an effusion of the Holy Spirit that sends thousands and thousands to their knees with tears in their eyes in brokenness before Him?

I keep reading my Bible, and I keep seeing my God, and the more I'm filled with love and passion for Him, the more I cannot shut down my desire to see Him work. I just can't limit my God. I can't do it. Each time I fix my eyes on my Saviour, I see the hope of the world and the source of all glory. Each time I find myself broken in worship and filled with awe of Him, my prayers grow larger and my faith grows with it. Each time I'm filled with the Holy Spirit of God, I'm overwhelmed with the grace of His gospel, and I so desperately want the world to have it as well. To boil it down, I simply can't stop asking *great* things from a God who can do *all* things. And revival is a great thing,

I have seen God do so much to ask too little of Him. I am well aware of the rampant sin of our world, and I know about all that the Bible says about the increasing evil of the last days. Is that going to dampen my passion for the greatest need in the history of the world, to hear the gospel of Jesus Christ? Is that going to cause me to give up, stay at home, and settle for a gospel that only resides in me? Or will I believe in my God for more? Will I believe Him for greater passion and joy and boldness in my life, and believe that He wants to extend that to others? Will I believe that as hard as the Christian life is promised to be, with it comes the fruit and power of the gospel?

I have faith and hope for this message. I have faith to believe that you have read this far and have an appetite for more. I have faith to believe that you are not okay with mediocrity, apathy, and complacency. I have faith to believe that you are sick and tired of just getting by in the Christian life, yawning your time away in front of the TV. I have faith to believe that you are starting to believe just how much God can do. I have faith to believe God can do much in you, in your family, in your church, and yes, in the world.

If only we would get our heads out of the sand of worldliness, we would realize just how much God is already doing across the earth. The darkness is powerful, but the light of the gospel is more powerful. Yes, Christians are dying for their faith today, but at the same time so many thousands are being regenerated to new life in Christ. In one sense Christians are dying, but in another sense the Church is thriving. Nothing and no can one stop Jesus Christ from building His Church. No one, not even the gates of hell (Matthew 16:18). So if the Church is guaranteed to advance through the power of the gospel, should we not want to get on board? This is one bus we don't want to miss.

## GET ON THE BUS

I remember vividly one of the first sermons I ever preached at my current church. It was on Matthew 16:18: *"I will build my church, and the gates of hell shall not prevail against it."* I pleaded with the people in those early days to accept the truth and power of this text. I remember saying to them something to the effect of "God is calling us to get on this bus, and we invite you to join us." I passionately implored them to get on board, believing it would be an incredible ride! Don't get me wrong, it has been hard and at times messy and filled with trials, but over a decade later the journey has been absolutely glorious. Thousands of changed lives, hundreds of baptisms, churches being planted, and multiplication all over the place—all to the glory of God.

The church I belong to was founded on a simple yet profound passion for the Lord and the premise that He wants to do more in us and through us. This is the bus we need to get on. It's a bus whose passengers are not satisfied spiritually, who are not content with little, but rather hungry for more of Christ and more of His glory to be seen. Yes, Lord, may it be so!

## IT'S TIME TO RE-DIG THE WELLS OF FAITH

These chapters issue a call for faith that leads to passion. It's a call for faith in what the Lord can do and what the Lord will do.

Years ago, I first set my eyes and heart upon a passage found in Genesis 26. It was another of those moments where the Word of God leapt from the page and landed upon my heart. I remember the chair I was sitting in at our kitchen table and the direction I was facing. I distinctly recall the joy that filled my heart. I was gripped by the Holy Spirit as He brought insight into God's Word. I was so deeply encouraged by the text and the metaphor it provided for our day of desperate need. Now, I know I'm not the first to see this truth, but it was one of those times when I felt like that I had uncovered new insight. I love those moments. They truly revive my faith, fuel my passion, and confirm my confidence that God speaks through His Word.

The passage came from Genesis 26:

*So Isaac departed from there and encamped in the Valley of Gerar and settled there. And Isaac dug again the wells of water that had been dug in the days of Abraham his father, which the Philistines had stopped after the death of Abraham. And he gave them the names that his father had given them.* (Genesis 26:17–18).

The reason this passage hit me so hard is the parallel it draws with the spiritual environment we find ourselves in. I believe so strongly that the Lord, from the beginning, has provided life-giving wells to His Church. These wells of living water have allowed the Church to exist and continue for two thousand years. When the Church, through faith, draws from these life-giving wells, it taps into a God-given, supernatural power that overcomes all obstacles and opposition. However, if the Church decides to move away from these God-given wells, the Church will be left to itself and its own devices. That will guarantee a

Church and a people who are empty, fruitless, ineffective, and dying of thirst.

I believe this is a clear answer to why the Church is largely so apathetic and complacent. We have resorted to relying on our own strategies and efforts instead of what God has supplied through the wells of faith. This cannot be. The enemy has so cleverly covered up the wells of faith. The enemy and our own sin of unbelief have distracted us from the true power of God. That is why we are being called back to faith, to passion, to re-dig the wells of faith that the Lord Himself has commanded us to drink from.

## ISAAC AND HIS SHOVEL

In Genesis 26:17–18, Isaac returned to the place where his father Abraham once dwelt, a place that contained wells of fresh, life-giving water that provided sustenance for the people of God. But notice that these wells were covered up by the enemy, the Philistines (Genesis 26:18). This, of course, was a smart move because if you take away the water, you essentially take away life.

Isaac, in a critical time of his life, needed to exercise faith, vision, and leadership. Spurred on by a famine (Genesis 26:1), he relocated his family and flock under the direction of the voice of God. Arriving in the valley of Gerar, Isaac knew where the wells of his father had been located, and he acted.

That sequence of awareness and action is such an important point. Isaac knew where the source of life was and he went after it. Do we in our day understand the true source of life and power in the Church? Many leaders will acknowledge truth with their mouths, yet say something different with their lives. There are also many leaders who refuse even to say the right things; they are capitulating to society, culture, and the fear of man.

However, Isaac knew that water was essential to survival, so he started to dig. These wells meant more than water; they were *springing* water. This was a constant supply of fresh, running water. These springs quenched the thirst of the people, but also the animals, the flocks, and the crops. The wells literally allowed the people of God to exist on that land.

*"And Isaac dug again the wells of water that has been dug in the days of Abraham his father…"* This is our call as much as ever. It's time to get out our shovels and get to work, by faith.

### YOU AND I MUST DIG

So here comes the spiritual and transforming principle for our day. Just as Isaac had to re-dig to survive, we too must re-dig the spiritual wells if we are going to survive and thrive as the Church. Think carefully about why so many churches are closing their doors across our nation. Why is there so little power and impact for Christ in so many areas? Why is fear gripping so many believers, and why are entire denominations a shell of what they were only fifty years ago? The answer is that the wells of faith have been covered and there is massive spiritual dehydration. Over time, the enemy has filled in the wells, and therefore the Church is literally dying of thirst. Help us, Lord!

Grab a shovel and dig. Don't give up. Don't stop. Dig until:

- •the Church uncovers the wells and preaches the Word of God with boldness.
- •the Church is captured by the kingdom of heaven.
- •the Church believes in the power of prayer.
- •the Church moves with conviction towards brokenness and dependence upon God.
- •the Church smashes their idols, repents, and moves out in Spirit-filled evangelism.

•the Church hears and receives the reality of living with a cost for Jesus Christ.

This kind of Church has uncovered the wells of faith and begun to drink from the all-satisfying, all-powerful living water of Jesus Christ. Here's what Warren Wiersbe says about this beautiful truth:

> Whenever there's been a revival of spiritual power in the history of the church, it's been because somebody has dug again the old wells so that God's life-giving Spirit can be free to work.[51]

Our goal is to be one of those somebodies!

Please understand that as we dig the spiritual wells of faith, we are digging out the grace of God. The life-giving water of the Lord always comes by the grace of God. This is not our effort ultimately, but it's a passion and longing for the grace and power that comes from the Lord. However, even though it's all God, we must ask, seek, and long for His grace upon our lives and within His Church.

## DO YOU BELIEVE?

Do you believe that God can bring a revival of spiritual power to your life? Do you believe that God can bring a revival of spiritual power to your family, your home, your church? Do you? Are you willing by faith to get out your spiritual shovel and dig out the wells of faith that truly give us life? Are you willing to see how the wells of faith have been covered up in your life and church? Now is the time to get your shovel, while we still have time.

Do you believe? I do. I believe that the Church today is being called to repent of the fear of man, to count the cost, and run towards the fear of God. I believe that the Church today must empty itself of temporary human ministry and fill itself with God-energized eternal life change. I believe that the Church today must abhor pride and pray for brokenness, humility, and meekness. I believe that the Church today must turn from timidity and implore God for the boldness that only comes from Him.

As we do this, we will find ourselves returning to the Source. Jesus is the Source of life, power, love, and revival. Here, the people of God, drinking from the wells of God, will share the heart of God—and that's where passion for Jesus Christ erupts.

## LIFE IS TOO SHORT NOT TO GROW IN CHRIST

As this book draws to a close, I want to reiterate my passion for passion. I have been called into ministry to see apathy replaced with fervency, for indifference to be replaced with conviction, and for complacency to be replaced with hunger. My heart grieves over the number of people who will stand before the Lord in the end and have to give an account for all the time wasted, talent squandered, and passion lavished on earthly things. What a tragedy it will be for those who in a fraction of a second will see the glory of the Lord and say, "I should've, could've, and would've." But then it will be too late.

If you're reading this, it's not too late! There is still time and the Lord has placed this message in your life to cause you to love and believe that life is too short not to grow in Christ. Life is too brief to waste it on anything apart from Christ. So take on the call for passion and the call for personal revival. Take on the conviction that by grace and through faith we will see personal and corporate momentum towards a true passion and longing for the things of God. Take up the challenge that as you begin to live out the themes of these pages, you will drink from the wells of faith.

I have seen time and time again that when the wells of faith are dug, the man is changed, the family is changed, and the church is changed. Again, hear me: life will not be easier this way, but it will be so much better. There is nothing like seeing the Spirit of God move powerfully through your life for His glory.

Life is too short not to grow in Christ, so let's continue to believe Him for more. The more I find myself in God's Word, loving God's Son and being filled with God's Spirit, the more I find a passion that truly satisfies. And it's here where I only want more. It's here where I can't stop asking great things from a God who can do all things.

Again, do you think God has reached a six out of ten with you and said, "That's good enough"? Think again. God Almighty has a passion for more in and through your life.

Shouldn't you?

# Endnotes

[1] J.C. Ryle, Practical Religion: Being Plain Papers on the Daily Duties, Experience, Dangers, and Privileges of Professing Christians (London, UK: W. Hunt Publishers, 1883), 199.

[2] Ibid., 184.

[3] Charles Spurgeon, "Morning and Evening—June 28," Teaching the Word Ministries. Date of access: November 23, 2015 (http://www.teachingtheword.org/apps/articles/web/articleid/60393/default.asp).

[4] To see the lyrics, visit http://www.christianlyricsonline.com/artists/dc-talk/in-the-light.html

[5] Charles Wesley, "And Can It Be that I Should Gain," 1738.

[6] A.W. Tozer, The Pursuit of God (Camp Hill, PA: Christian Publications, 1982), 6.

[7] C.T. Studd (1860–1931) was an athlete and missionary pastor known for these lines, which he lived out.

[8] John Piper, Filling Up the Afflictions of Christ (Wheaton, IL: Crossway, 2009), 67.

[9] A.W. Tozer, The Pursuit of God (Camp Hill, PA: Christian Publications, 1982), 6.

[10] C.S. Lewis, The Weight of Glory (New York, NY: Simon & Schuster, 1980), 26.

[11] L.B. Cowman, Streams in the Desert, Volume One (Grand Rapids, MI: Zondervan, 1996), 8–9. Quoting Charles Spurgeon. Emphasis added.

[12] A.W. Tozer, The Pursuit of God (Camp Hill, PA: Christian Publications, 1982), 15.

[13] J.C. Ryle, "Christian Zeal." Date of access: November 15, 2015 (http://www.biblebb.com/files/ryle/zeal.htm).

[14] H.C.G. Moule, Charles Simeon (London, UK: InterVarsity, 1948), 133–134.

[15] A.W. Tozer, The Root of the Righteous (Camp Hill, PA: Wing Spread Publishers, 2006), 157.

[16] John Piper, The Roots of Endurance (Wheaton, IL: Crossway, 2002), 109.

[17] C.S. Lewis, Mere Christianity, (New York, NY: MacMillan Publishing Company, 1960), 106.

[18] Arnold Dallimore, George Whitefield: The Life and Times of the Great Evangelist of the Eighteenth-Century Revival (Carlisle, PA: Banner of Truth, 1970).

[19] Iain Murray, Heroes (Carlisle, PA: Banner of Truth, 2009), 80.

[20] Ibid.

[21] Ibid., 56.

[22] Horatio Spafford, "It Is Well with My Soul," 1876.

[23] C.S. Lewis, The Last Battle (London, UK: William Collins Sons & Co., 1980), 162.

[24] R.T. Kendall, The Complete Guide to the Parables: Understanding and Applying the Stories of Jesus (Grand Rapids, MI: Revel, 2004), 261.

[25] John Piper, Twitter post, March 7, 2015, 10:01 a.m. (https://twitter.com/johnpiper/status/574268756148502528).

[26] Steve J. Miller, D.L. Moody on Spiritual Leadership (Chicago, IL: Moody Publisher, 2004), 160.

[27] R.T. Kendall, The Complete Guide to the Parables: Understanding and Applying the Stories of Jesus (Grand Rapids, MI: Revel, 2004), 261.

[28] Harold Burchett, Bright Light: A Lifetime of Seeing God at Work (Wakefield, RI: Bringing Christ Back Ministries, 2013), xi.

[29] Ibid.

[30] Erroll Hulse and David Kingdon, ed., A Marvelous Ministry: How the All-Round Ministry of Charles Haddon Spurgeon Speaks to Us Today (Ligonier, PA: Soli Deo Gloria Publications, 1993), 128.

[31] David Paul Tripp, Dangerous Calling (Wheaton, IL: Crossway, 2012), 41.

[32] William Cowper, "There Is a Fountain Filled with Blood," 1772.

[33] ESV Study Bible (Wheaton, IL: Crossway, 2008), 2505.

[34] I have personally been using the Robert Murray McCheyne reading plan for years now, but that's only one option among many. On our church website, we provide several reading plans to choose from (www.harvestoakville.ca/resources/bible-reading-plans).

[35] E.M. Bounds, The Complete Works of E.M. Bounds on Prayer (Grand Rapids, MI: Baker Books, 1990), 39.

[36] Ibid.

[37] Ibid., 40.

[38] Martyn Lloyd-Jones, Preaching and Preachers (Grand Rapids, MI: Zondervan, 1971), 170–171.

[39] David Eby, Power Preaching for Church Growth: The Role of Preaching in Growing Churches (Ross-shire, UK: Mentor Imprint, 2009), 57.

[40] George MacDonald, Edge-Tools of Speech (Boston, MA: Ticknor and Company, 1886), 384.

[41] John Calvin, Institutes of Christian Religion (Westminster, UK: John Knox Press, 2006), 108.

[42] Found at: Anonymous, "Larry Burkett on financial advice for the second half of your life," Life Coach for God. July 26th, 2012. http://verticallivingministries.com/tag/the-story-of-mr-and-mrs-thing/

[43] George MacDonald, Edge-Tools of Speech (Boston, MA: Ticknor and Company, 1886), 384.

[44] Steve Miller, C.H. Spurgeon on Spiritual Leadership (Chicago, IL: Moody Publishers, 2003), 165.

[45] Ibid.

[46] John Piper, The Swans Are Not Silent (Wheaton, IL: Crossway, 2009). I wholeheartedly recommend this series to anyone desiring a greater passion for the Lord. The examples and testimonies provide a tremendous encouragement in boldness, perseverance, and all-out love for Christ. In terms of a passion for souls, I particularly recommend Book Five, Filling Up the Afflictions of Christ.

[47] Ibid.

[48] John Piper, Filling Up with Afflictions of Christ (Wheaton, IL: Crossway, 2009), 81.

[49] Lyle W. Dorsett, A Passion for Souls: The Life of D.L. Moody (Chicago, IL: Moody Publishers, 1997), 21.

[50] Leonard Ravenhill, "Quotes." Date of access: November 25, 2015 (http://www.leonard-ravenhill.com/quotes).

[51] Warren Wiersbe, The Bible Exposition Commentary: Pentateuch (Colorado Springs, CO: Victor, 2001), 119.